Broad Norfolk

Broad Norfolk

by

JONATHAN MARDLE

with illustrations

by

LEE

PROSPECT PRESS

Prospect Press
Norwich

© Wensum Books 1973
© George Nobbs and Native Guides Ltd 2003

ISBN 0-9545521-0-5

CONTENTS

LIST OF ILLUSTRATIONS

AUTHOR'S ACKNOWLEDGEMENT

My first acknowledgement must be to the *Eastern Daily Press*, for which I have written for more than forty years—thus gaining the experience of Norfolk on which much of this book is based. Moreover, a good deal of the present *Broad Norfolk* is drawn from a previous book under the same title, which I edited for that newspaper in 1949.

I am also grateful to many old friends—some of whom are now, alas, dead—for the knowledge I have derived from their letters and conversation about the Norfolk dialect. The letters, extending over a period of more than twenty years, have been most valuable. Where I have drawn upon books, I have made due acknowledgement in the text. I thank my colleague Mervyn Payne, who kindly read the manuscript and made some valuable suggestions.

I would also like to thank George Nobbs and Alan Dean of Wensum Books for asking me to write this work for them. They have already published a number of excellent books of local interest and I am grateful to them for their help and encouragement.

It would be useless to try to write a new *Vocabulary of East Anglia* in 1973, when the much richer nineteenth-century vocabularies of Moor, Forby, and Nall are available to those who wish to study the dialect in greater depth. I have, however, appended a list of Norfolk words I know or believe to have been current during the past fifty years.

Finally, and most warmly, I have to thank my collaborator, Joe Lee—a Yorkshireman who, after thirty-two years of making London laugh over its *Evening News*, has retired to Norwich to make Norfolk laugh. Nowadays he illuminates the *Eastern Daily Press* with his political cartoons, but this is only one of his many interests. I never knew, until I persuaded him to illustrate this book, how much he had absorbed of the *genius loci* as well as the malt liquor of Norfolk.

But when a celebrated London cartoonist also turns, as he has, to painting in water-colours, I know that the influence of the Norwich School has got hold of him. There is, however, a difference. Few of the Norwich School could draw people. Lee can.

Norwich
July 1973

Jonathan Mardle

Jonathan . . . mardling.

I

THE NORFOLK LANGUAGE

'Ha' yar fa'r got a dickey, bor?'

A Norfolk nurse during the First World War, thinking she recognized a wounded soldier as coming from her own village, tested him by whispering this question in his ear. And the wounded man chuckled, and mumbled from among his bandages:

'Yis, an' he want a fule to roide 'um. Will yew come?'

The dialect is not so strong now as it was sixty years ago, but Norfolk people, when they meet each other in strange places, are still apt to make a recognition signal of the question, which means, 'Has your father got a donkey, boy?' and the retort, 'Yes, and he wants a fool to ride him. Will you come?'

And after that little ceremony is over, it is likely that the compatriots will recite, with an exaggerated Norfolk 'drant', or drawl, the incantation: 'A-a-all the wa-a-ay ter Swa-a-affham, t'ree days tro-o-oshin', an' all for na-a-athin'.' Then they will laugh, not because 'All the way to Swaffham, three days' threshing, and all for nothing' is much of a joke in itself, but because, long drawn out, it is Norfolk people's favourite caricature of their own dialect.

Moreover, Norfolk people are also marked by their habit of addressing all and sundry as 'bor'. Scholars have argued at length whether 'bor' is derived from 'boy', 'neighbour', or some more obscure Anglo-Saxon word, but nobody has come to any firm conclusion about it. It remains a fact that East Anglians address all their masculine friends and acquaintances as 'bor'. Sometimes the term is applied to women, too, but they are more commonly called 'maw', which is an abbreviation of 'mawther'. And a stranger might think 'mawther' meant 'mother', until he heard a little girl, or even a baby in arms, spoken of as 'the little mawther'. It is the East Anglian term for all womankind.

Being written in Norfolk, and by a Norfolk man, this book is called *Broad Norfolk*, but the dialect is in fact East Anglian. It has been claimed with some justification that, at any rate until the end of the First World War, it was almost a separate language. It was spoken, with local variations, all over Norfolk and Suffolk, and in the greater part of Essex—until to the southward it was submerged under Cockney, and to the westward it changed by subtle gradations into the different dialect of the Fens. The Reverend Robert Forby (1759–1825) wrote a *Vocabulary of East Anglia* which is still the standard work on the subject, and he observed that if at that time a countryman from the shores of the Wash had met another from the banks of the Orwell they would have understood one another perfectly, but if they had been joined by a third man from north of the Humber they would have found him incomprehensible, neither would he have understood them.

Forby was born at Stoke Ferry, in West Norfolk, went to school at King's Lynn, became a Fellow of Caius College, Cambridge, and then returned as a clergyman to the same district from which he sprang—where the gentle undulations of what Fenmen call 'High Norfolk' slope towards the flat basin of the Great Ouse. He spent most of his uneventful life as Rector of Fincham, where he combined the duties of a parson with those of a magistrate and a

'Ha' yar fa'r got a dickey, bor?'   *See* page 11.

tutor of private pupils, and made a hobby of what he called his 'Icenian Glossary'. He supplemented his own knowledge with notes from numerous correspondents in other parts of Norfolk and in Suffolk and Essex.

His *Vocabulary of East Anglia* was not published until 1830—five years after his death. It contains about 2,000 words and phrases. Not all of them are peculiar to East Anglia. Some are good Old English which has persisted in country speech in many other parts of the country since Shakespeare's time, or indeed Chaucer's. For instance, 'dodman' is Norfolk for a snail (in Suffolk it is 'hodmandod'), but there is a Dodman Point in Cornwall, where the humped promontory is named after its likeness to a snail.

And Broad Norfolk or Suffolk, to this day, can elucidate Shakespearian words which are otherwise inexplicable. Hamlet, hinting to Guildenstern that he is not so mad as he pretends to be, says, 'I am but mad north-north-west; when the wind is southerly, I know a hawk from a handsaw.' Which sounds utter nonsense. But a Norfolk man knows the text is mistaken. What Shakespeare must have written was not 'handsaw' but 'harnser' or 'harnsey', which to this day is good East Anglian for a heron. The late R. W. Ketton-Cremer found, in the margin of his copy of Forby, a note of a remark made by a country boy in 1860: 'I well remember my father used to read to us out of a right ancient book, how every gentleman in Norfolk rode about with a hawk perked on his wrist, and they used to hawk at them there harnseys and lead 'em a rare life.' So Shakespeare meant Hamlet to say, 'I know a hawk from a harnser'—which any Elizabethan sportsman would have understood.

In a long and learned introduction to his *Vocabulary of East Anglia*, Forby noticed, in lighter vein, some East Anglian peculiarities which are not so much part of the dialect as of the local character and turn of phrase. For instance, there is the way of stringing words together into picturesque adjectives, like a woman who appeared before Forby's bench of magistrates to give evidence against a ne'er-do-well who had run away from Fincham, leaving several illegitimate children chargeable to the parish. She said he was a 'toss-potly, stuff-gutly, smoke-bacca-ly, starve-bastardly, whoremongerly wagabond'.

Much of Forby's Introduction, however, dealt with etymology and the derivations of East Anglian words. This is a dangerous subject except for specialists. The present writer does not propose to meddle with it, except to remark that the low-lying, rounded bulge of the Norfolk and Suffolk coast into the North Sea has been much subject to invasions—some martial and some peaceful—and that each wave of invaders, settling down and eventually mixing with its predecessors, contributed something to the dialect of East Anglia. Fundamentally, it is Anglo-Saxon: the Germanic language of the invaders from the Netherlands, North Germany, and Jutland who, from about the year 400, overwhelmed the previous Romano-British civilization. It is said that the homely word 'dwile', which a Norfolk woman still uses for the cloth with which she wipes up what she calls a 'swidge' of water on the floor, is one of the most familiar examples of a survival in the dialect from the Anglo-Saxons. Moreover, you will also find it on the other side of the North Sea: for if in modern Holland you are clumsy enough to upset your glass the waiter will fetch a *dweil* to wipe up the mess.

In the ninth century the Danes invaded the East Coast, and martyred the Christian King Edmund of East Anglia, who is still commemorated by the remains of the great Abbey of Bury St Edmunds. I have heard that old people in East Norfolk used to call the carrion-crow 'Harra the Denchman' (Harold the Danish man), which suggests a very long folk-memory of the Anglo-Saxons' terror of the heathen Vikings.

13

East Anglia became part of the Danelaw. The Danes, who came to plunder and remained to farm, intermingled with the Anglo-Saxons, and settled here in such numbers that by the time of the Norman Conquest East Anglia was the most thickly populated part of England. The names of the villages in the Fleggs, north of Great Yarmouth, and in between the Broads and the sea—names like Ormesby, Rollesby, Filby, and Stokesby—suggest by the Scandinavian termination 'by' how densely the Vikings settled along the East Coast. At Lowestoft the word 'score'—for the steep lanes down the cliffs to the beach—is of the same Norse origin as the Yorkshire word 'scar' for a cliff. So Danish became mixed with Saxon as part of the East Anglian dialect: just as, in the larger sense, it became part of the Anglo-Saxon which by Chaucer's time had been fused along with Norman French and monkish Latin into English.

The next contribution to the mixed population of East Anglia, and hence to its dialect, came more peacefully from Flanders, by way of the Flemish weavers, who were encouraged by Edward III and his Queen, Philippa of Hainault, to settle here in the fourteenth century, and thus to found a great trade in English cloth, rather than export English wool to be spun and woven by the more sophisticated craftsmen of the Low Countries.

From this period dates the great handicraft worsted weaving industry, which founded the fortunes of Norwich and Norfolk. It remains a matter of historical and etymological dispute whether the now-small village of Worstead in Norfolk—with its medieval church almost the size of a cathedral—gave its name to the cloth, or the cloth to the village, or whether both names were of different origin. At all events, the trade flourished richly. It temporarily flagged in the middle of the sixteenth century, but was revived from 1564 onwards, when Elizabeth I encouraged a fresh influx of skilled Dutch and Walloon weavers— Protestant refugees from Spanish persecution in Flanders and the Netherlands—to settle in Norwich and improve its manufactures with their 'new stuffs'. They came in such numbers that by the beginning of the seventeenth century it was reckoned that one-third of the population of Norwich was of foreign origin. The majority spoke Dutch and a minority French—but, like previous invaders, they intermarried with the local population and eventually became indistinguishable from them. Their skill gave such a fresh impetus to trade in Norwich that it became the second city of England after London, and so remained until it was outstripped towards the end of the eighteenth century by the Industrial Revolution in the Midlands and the North.

It is a nice conjecture, how much of the Anglo-Saxon element in the East Anglian dialect was derived from the original Anglo-Saxons, and how much came at second hand, as it were, through the Dutch of the sixteenth century 'Strangers', as they were called. However, I fancy it may have been from the French-speaking Walloons among them—or from a smaller influx of Huguenots, driven out of France in the seventeenth century by the Revocation of the Edict of Nantes—that we got the word 'lucom', meaning an attic window, or one of those hooded projections from old mills and warehouses where sacks of grain were hoisted by a pulley and chain to the top floor. The word is obviously derived from the French *lucarne*. I have also read that down to the eighteenth century, when the sanitary arrangements of Norwich were very primitive indeed, and housewives used to empty the slops out of the upper windows of the old overhanging houses into the 'cockeys' (drains) that ran down the middle of the narrow cobbled streets, they used to shout 'gardiloo' (*garde à vous*) to warn people in the street below. 'Plancher'—old Norfolk for floor—is again of French origin, and so, I used to think, was 'mardle' (*mardelle*), which means a

14

'Gardiloo!'   *See* page 14.

'pond', but has a second meaning of 'gossip'—presumably from the gossip that went on around the village water-supply. At all events, I adopted it in that sense, years ago, as a pen-name to use in the *Eastern Daily Press*, and added Jonathan because it was a Christian name that seemed to sound right with Mardle. But recently a learned woman correspondent to the *Eastern Daily Press*, who has studied Anglo-Saxon, has told me 'mardle' (as gossip) has a much older origin. She says Beowulf 'mardled'.

Norfolk people are known as 'Norfolk dumplings'. This is nothing to do with their shape, but with what is alleged to be their favourite article of diet. A Norfolk dumpling or 'swimmer' is made of flour, water, and yeast, and 'swims' on top of the broth or stew in which it is cooked. A good cook can make it as light as a feather. But I am afraid that what Norfolk dumplings really reflect is the poverty of the county during the nineteenth century.

The surviving inn sign of the 'Plough and Shuttle' at Marsham is a reminder that at least until the end of the eighteenth century the Norfolk towns and villages had two strings to their bow—agriculture and weaving. Moreover, the earnings of a farm-hand were often augmented by those of his wife and children, who spun yarn for the weaving trade; and he also had his rights on the common land to supplement his wages.

At the beginning of the nineteenth century the greater part of the old handicraft weaving trade was lost to the power-looms of the North of England, and at the same time the Enclosures deprived the farm-labourer of the little measure of independence he had enjoyed from the common land. Thenceforward, he was ill-paid when at work, and half-starved when out of work. At the same time, the weavers and spinners were bitterly impoverished. So Norfolk dumplings eked out some very thin broth.

However, Major Christopher Bush—who under the pseudonym 'Michael Home' wrote the Breckland classic, *God and the Rabbit*—once told me that the dumplings he knew as a boy in Breckland in the 1890s were made of a savoury mixture of chopped pork and onions enclosed in a suet crust. But this was in the family of a village tradesman and smallholder.

Whereas the inhabitants of Norfolk are called 'dumplings', Suffolk people have the even less flattering name of 'Silly Suffolk'; but there are apologists who say the adjective was originally the Old English 'seely', meaning holy. Fenmen are known as 'yellow-bellies', that is frogs, and are also alleged to have webbed feet.

It is remarkable that it was not until the latter part of the seventeenth century that anybody took notice in writing of the fact that Norfolk had a dialect. Then the learned and inquisitive Sir Thomas Browne, the author of *Religio Medici*, who was a Londoner before Norwich claimed him as one of its greatest citizens, made a list in his little tract *Of Languages, and particularly of the Saxon tongue* of twenty-six examples of 'words of no general reception in England but of common use in Norfolk'. Some of them were obsolete by the time Robert Forby got to work on his *Vocabulary of East Anglia* more than a hundred years later, but others, like 'bunny' (for a bruise or swelling), 'mawther' (for a woman or girl), 'seele' (for example, 'I gave him the *seal* o' the day'), 'stingy' (meaning cruel or mean), 'thepes', 'thapes', or 'fapes' (meaning green gooseberries), 'sibrits' (banns), and 'paxwax' (the sinew in a joint of meat) are still current Norfolk, or were so in my boyhood.

Forby, in the 1820s, thought the principal value of his book was as a record of a dialect that was bound to die out with the advance of education and the improvement of communications as he saw them, even during the Regency. He deplored the affectation of a village girl who presented a lady with a 'numbarel'—he thought newfangled words like 'umbrella' ought to have no place in a villager's vocabulary.

He was justified to the extent that no subsequent work has superseded or greatly enlarged upon his *Vocabulary of East Anglia* and Major Moor's *Suffolk Words and Phrases* (which came out in 1823). John Greaves Nall added words peculiar to the seafaring and fishing community to the Glossary in his *History of Yarmouth, Lowestoft and their Fisheries* (1886), but the rest of Nall's Glossary was based upon Forby and Moor.

In 1893 the *Eastern Daily Press* published a booklet called *Broad Norfolk*, which was a collection of 125 letters to the paper concerning the dialect. Harry Cozens-Hardy, who edited the booklet, prophesied with regret that this might be the last manifestation of a dialect that was bound to die out within the next generation under the influence of the Board Schools. But in 1949—after the upheaval caused by two world wars, and in spite of the influences of State education, the cinema, and broadcasting—there was a second and even more striking demonstration of interest by Norfolk people in their own dialect, in the shape of 420 letters written to the *Eastern Daily Press* within a couple of months—all about Broad Norfolk. It then fell to the present writer to collect these letters into a second *Broad Norfolk* booklet, which was sold out as soon as published.

Today, you can often hear nearly as many Midland or London as Norfolk accents in the streets of Norwich, Great Yarmouth, King's Lynn, or Thetford. We are told the population of East Anglia is growing—largely by immigration from other parts of the country—at a faster rate than that of any other English region. And yet the new 'Strangers' seem as interested as the natives in the peculiar dialect of the province in which they have settled, and there is a demand for a third *Broad Norfolk*, which this book is intended to satisfy.

II

THE SOUND OF NORFOLK

There are three elements in dialect—the pronunciation and accent, the vocabulary, and the peculiar local grammar and turn of phrase. Of these, the vocabulary is the most perishable. It weakens, and undoubtedly has weakened in East Anglia, as the old operations of hand labour and horse-traction, to which much of it refers, have died out. The pronunciation and accent, and the turn of phrase, are more lasting, although I am certain Broad Norfolk is not nearly so 'broad' today as it was sixty years ago—and when I read Norfolk as it was written by people like Forby and Nall in the nineteenth century I feel sure some of the distinctive vowel sounds have changed, and the dialect does not sound the same now as it did then.

However, you have only to listen at the gates of any school—grammar or otherwise—to know that, in spite of all the efforts of schoolmasters and schoolmistresses, and all the imitations of the Mid-Atlantic accents of disc-jockeys, the remains of Broad Norfolk are still very substantial indeed. An insuperable difficulty in writing about it is that it is impossible, except by the use of phonetic symbols understood only by philologists, to reproduce in writing the sound of Norfolk. One can only try, inadequately, to suggest the pronunciation. Even so, the peculiar up-and-down of the intonation, which in Suffolk becomes a sing-song, is left out. It has been said, rather flatteringly, that Broad Suffolk is Norfolk set to music.

But I do not think even its best friends could justly call the East Anglian dialect musical. We are a very reticent people, who do not find it easy to sing, or to act upon the stage. It is said that the prevailing east wind makes us reluctant to open our mouths: we swallow our consonants and do strange things with our vowels.

The sound of a Norfolk 'a'—usually rendered in writing as 'aa'—was correctly described by Forby as 'like the bleating of a very young lamb'. It rhymes with 'air' or 'care', but it is long drawn out, as in 'Oopen yew that gaate, maate, dew yew'll be tew laate.' A long 'e', on the other hand, is sometimes changed into an 'a', so that 'beer' becomes 'bare', or three 'cheers' turn into three 'chairs'. But, most confusingly, 'a' sometimes becomes 'e', so that a chair that you sit on is a 'cheer'.

Short 'e' often becomes short 'i', as in 'Git you out o' the way', or 'I ent a-gorn hoome, not yit I ent', or it can turn into short 'u', as in 'shud' for 'shed'. Long 'i' tends to sound like 'oi'—'He was a-roidin' o' his boike down the loke, toime he see the gal Mary a' the t'other soide o' the hedge.'

But that which above all betrays a Norfolk man—strive as he may, having risen in the world, to assume an Oxford or B.B.C. accent—is his incapacity to deal with a round 'o'. In moments of stress he will always say 'I hoop' instead of 'I hope'. He 'oopens' the door, and he washes his hands with 'soup'.

Neither is this the end of the tricks the Norfolk tongue plays with 'o'. A road in Norfolk is a 'rood', and rhymes with wood or hood. But a long 'o' can turn into a 'u', so that the

18

moon is the 'mune', and a fool is 'a duzzy fule', and do is 'du' or 'dew' (whichever way you choose to spell it). A short 'o' can become a long 'a'—as in 'naathin' for 'nothing'.

'Du different', in behaviour as well as pronunciation, is said to be the strongest local characteristic—so much so that the new University of East Anglia took 'Do different' for its motto. And Broad Norfolk also does different with its 'u's'. The sound of a Norfolk long 'u' has been compared with that of a French one. Whereas refined ladies are inclined to pronounce the word 'beautiful' as 'byootiful', a Norfolk woman says 'tha's bu'iful'.

Boy becomes 'booy', as in the old village tradesman's summing up of the value of boys as apprentices:

One booy is half a man,
Tew booys are half a booy,
T'ree booys ain't no booy at all.

'Ow', as in out, is a very blunt sound in East Norfolk, but in the West, as you come into the Fens, it sharpens into 'eout'—and this is the beginning of the transition, in Cambridge-shire, into a different dialect.

'Don't' in Norfolk becomes 'dorn't'—'I dorn't know naathin' about that.' Similarly, 'going' becomes 'gorn'—we say, 'I aren't a-gorn to du it.' But when we say, 'I won't do it', we drop the 'w' and say, 'I 'oon't du it.'

Except in Norwich—which has developed a slipshod urban argot that is different from, and inferior to, old-fashioned country Norfolk—we do not in general drop our 'h's', but the older generation has a habit, like Dickens's Cockneys, of substituting 'w' for 'v'. A man will say, 'I'm a-gorn hoome arter my wittles'—meaning his victuals, or in other words, food. And the wind-vane on the masts of the old Norfolk wherries was called the 'wane'.

We are, however, inclined to maltreat many of our other consonants—particularly the 't's'—by leaving them out altogether. On the other hand, sometimes 'th' becomes a hard 't', as when we count 'one, tew, t'ree, fower, foive'. But most of our median and final 'r's' are apt, like the 't's', to disappear—no Norfolk man can roll an 'r'.

An extreme example of the neglect of consonants and general tendency to run words into one another is illustrated by the man who comes up to a group of his friends, blowing hard through an empty pipe, and asks, 'Ha' ya' go' 'na bacca onya inny onya?'—which means, 'Have you got any tobacco on you, any of you?'

As for Broad Norwich, it has at its worst degenerated into an adenoidal gabble, which schoolmasters justly deplore. A stranger once came up to me in Norwich's London Street and asked the way to 'Largo Lane'. I was puzzled, and was about to say I had never heard of it, when suddenly the light dawned, and I realized that the stranger had been directed in Broad Norwich to Lower Goat Lane, which the Norwich tongue would have distorted into 'La'r Goo' Lay'.

A Norwich child will ask for 'a bi' o' bre'n bu'a' when it wants a piece of bread and butter. An aggrieved schoolmaster once made a list of such phrases that he had heard from his pupils, and it was afterwards suggested that 'Asswahreesay' (That's what he says) might be adopted as a name for the peculiar language spoken in Norwich. Here is the rest of the list:

'Wossuponya?'—What is the matter with you?
'In'agora'durt'—I'm not going to do it.
'Corrumahr!'—Goodness! I'm hot!

19

'Cummupair Mairble'—Come up here, Mabel.
'Wossairdurn?'—What is he doing?
'Ayyadunna?'—Have you done it?
'Inchagart?'—Haven't you got it?
'Eewahravalillarna'—He wants to have a little of it.
'Gurza'—Give it to me.
'Owdsi'eegirron?'—How did the City get on?
'Cummair'—Come here.
'Woyyawahn?'—What do you want?

The schoolmaster argued that it was surely right to substitute standard English for such a horrid jargon. But if he were a Norwich man he would have to be careful lest his own tongue betrayed him, as it did another teacher who was trying to drill his class in spoken English.

'Don't say "be'er" ', he said, 'Say "bet-ter".'

'Bet-ter', repeated the class, carefully.

'Ah!' said the teacher, 'Tha's be'er!'

III

NORFOLK WORDS

As I have said before, vocabulary is the part of a dialect that perishes most quickly, as the old customs, processes, materials, and implements, to which it refers, die out. Not many people now remember that a 'dutfin' was the bridle of a cart-horse, nor that he drew the plough or harrow by means of a 'swingle-bar'—neither does anybody, in compensation, invent special local words for the parts of a tractor or the machinery of a combine-harvester.

That most perceptive writer and anthropologist, George Ewart Evans, who began his studies of rural Suffolk just after the Second World War, has shown in *Ask the Fellows who Cut the Hay* (1956) and in his other books that a separate and age-old rural culture began to die out of provinces like East Anglia in the first ten or twenty years of the present century, and is now recoverable only through the oral tradition preserved in the memories and beliefs of very old people. Indeed, the half-magical lore of the old team-men, which Evans describes in *The Horse in the Furrow* (1960), would never have been confided to him if the old men to whom he spoke had not been conscious that theirs was a dying craft. I was reminded, when I read it, of an old man who told me years ago that right down to about 1900 Back St Stephen's Street, in Norwich, was the residence of certain 'wise men and women'—white witches—who were consulted like regular medical or veterinary practitioners by country people coming up to market on Saturdays. There is nothing left of Back St Stephen's Street now excepting the back premises of supermarkets.

Similarly, I was not sure, when I was editing a previous *Broad Norfolk* for the *Eastern Daily Press* in 1949, whether the writers of the letters of which the booklet was composed were writing Norfolk words that were still in use, or words that they remembered to have been used when they were young. Still less am I sure about the currency of the examples I give now. But I have come across some remarkable survivals into the 1970s. For instance a Scots doctor asked me quite recently why the triangle of grass at the junction of two Norfolk lanes was called 'the haater piece'. The term was new to me, but I found out that it was 'the heater piece'—so called because it was the same shape as the triangular pieces of iron that were heated in the fire, and then picked up with tongs and put inside the box-irons with which Victorian women ironed their linen. I should think it must be at least sixty years since this was a common practice—box-irons are now museum exhibits—yet someone giving a direction to my doctor friend told him to turn left at 'the haater piece'.

I wonder whether anybody still says that a thundery sky (or, for that matter, a dirty face) is 'as black as the hakes'—the 'hakes' being the hooks from which cooking-pots were hung over an open fire. I suppose the continued use of 'dwiles' to wipe up 'swidges' from the floor indicates that the mechanization of housewifery has not yet gone so far as that of industry. But I should warn people that the game of 'flonking the dwile'—nowadays accepted by many visitors to country fêtes as some kind of traditional Norfolk sport—is not genuine folklore. It was invented after the Second World War by a group of sportive young farmers —with a cloth, a pole, and a pail of beer—as a send-up of folklore. The now middle-aged

As black as the hakes. *See* page 21.

inventors must find it the cream of the joke that 'dwile-flonking' is now accepted as the genuine article.

The real old Norfolk had rougher sports. For instance, the Camping Ground at Swaffham commemorates a crude sort of football that used to be played between teams of anything up to a hundred a side, with no rules about fouls. Boxing, wrestling, and hacking were all part of the game of camping, which was abandoned early in the nineteenth century because it caused too many serious injuries and even deaths. There was also a Norfolk form of wrestling which consisted of two men gripping one another by the shoulders and then hacking at each other's shins with their hobnailed boots until one of them fell down.

Among gentler games, children's games, I love 'tittermatorter' for see-saw: it is one of those words that describes exactly what it means. 'Huckabuck' is leapfrog. Equally delightful is 'bishy-barneybee' for a ladybird.

> *Bishy bishy-barneybee*
> *Tell me when your wedding be.*
> *If it be tomorrow day*
> *Flap your wings and fly away.*

But 'arpintood', put to me by a friend to puzzle me, was a term in nature that defeated me until I was told the circumstances. It was said by a mower, pointing to a frog that had hopped out of the long grass, and the word was 'hopping toad'. For Norfolk dialect recognizes three kinds of toad—a frog, which is a 'hopping toad', a natterjack, which is a 'running toad', and a toad properly so called, which is a 'crawling toad'. A frog is also called a 'fresher'.

Toads were credited—as by the witches in *Macbeth*—with magical properties. Their desiccated remains are sometimes found in the chimneys of old houses, where they were put in the belief that the person who had been ill-wished would wither away even as the toad's body withered in the heat of the chimney. It is not so very long ago since an old Norfolk man, who had gone right off his game on the bowling-green, said irritably, 'I dorn't know what ha' gone wrong. That fare as if I can't do naathin' right. I reckon someone must ha' put the toods on me.'

The old gentleman was 'in a puckaterry' (purgatory). That is, he was in a muddle and a temper. So, as it was a hot day and he was 'all of a muckwash' (sweating) he sat down in the 'swale' (shade), only to find he had sat on a 'pishamares' [ants'] nest'. He 'wholly mobbed' (scolded).

The word 'wholly' is important in the Norfolk vocabulary. It is used for emphasis. For instance, the weather can be 'wholly hot' or 'wholly cold'. An angry man is 'wholly riled', and a frightened one is 'wholly scared'. 'Fare' is also important. A bullock that fails to put on flesh, or a human invalid who is slow to recover, 'dorn't fare to moise' (improve) and on a 'daggly' (damp) day it 'fare to mizzle' (drizzle). A man who feels out of sorts will tell you he 'dorn't fare noo matters', also, 'he dorn't feel wery fierce'.

There is a large vocabulary of violence, which suggests that our forefathers must have been a rough lot. 'Thacking', 'troshing', 'koishing', 'soling', and 'twilting' all mean thrashing. A 'clout' is a blow, a 'ding o'-the lug' is a smack on the ear, and 'a Swar'ston winder' (Swardeston window) is a black eye. When children cried as a result of these inflictions they 'blaa-ed' or 'winnicked' (whimpered). In either event they were likely to be told unsympathetically, 'Dew yew hold yar row, an' stop kickin' up a duller' (noise). And when they had

Bishy bishy-barneybee. *See* page 23.

been reduced to silence, it would be, 'Now, dorn't yew dast [dare] make a deen [sound].'
Children could ill afford, in those days, to be 'mure-hearted' ('demure-' or tender-hearted).

The Norfolk medical vocabulary is even more weird and wonderful. When a Norfolk man is sick he 'feels quare', and his friends do not help when they tell him 'Yew look right lantern-jawed.' Perhaps he is 'under the doctor'. If he has a cough it is a 'tizzick', and if this does not mend he may become 'bronnical', or even 'git the pumony'. If he is feverish he 'dudders' (shivers).

But a shiver, in Broad Norfolk, means a splinter in your finger, which may be covered with a 'hutkin' (finger-stall). A boil is a 'push'—Nall quotes the following description of the distressing results of a push: 'Ta itch, an' ta pritch [pricks], an' ta galver [throbs].' 'That bulk' and 'that gruckle' are other descriptions of throbbing. To 'grane' a man means to strangle him. To 'quackle' also means to throttle, but the complaint need not always be taken seriously. A farmer, putting on a stiff collar on Sunday morning, said, 'That fare to quackle me.'

A doctor once got a call to an old countryman in these terms: 'He's wholly bad with a abser [abscess] an' tha's a-suin' [discharging]. He fared to git up in the night, but he shruck out wi' the misery o' his grind [groin]. He can't come down to yew, du he 'oon't never git there. Come yew today, doctor, please: doon't, he'll die.'

This is a description of an accident to a horseman: 'Ol' George, he fare wholly quare today. The old hoss, that jammed [trod] onter his toe yisterda' mornin'. My heart, that give him some clorth [pain].'

In childbirth, midwifery is called 'nijjerting', and the 'midnight woman' (midwife) is said to be 'gorn a-nijjertin'. A man once went into a chemist's and said, 'I want some pills wot'll hull my missus into a sweat.'

So our doctors have to learn the language. Dr Irene Green, when newly come to Norfolk from Durham, was consulted by a woman who said, 'I want some med'cine for my little 'un. Pore little booy, he suffer suthin' terrible from stoppages.'

Thinking the malady must be constipation, Dr Green prescribed a laxative, only for the mother to complain a week later: 'Doctor, that there med'cine ent done him a mite o' good. All that fare to du is gripe him.'

The doctor then discovered that 'stoppages' was the Norfolk term for fits—and, she says, as a definition of what happens in a fit, it is not a bad description, at that.

In old Norfolk, a perambulator was known as a 'cooch' (coach), and the mother did not push it, she 'crowded' it. Similarly, a gardener 'crowds' his wheelbarrow, and a dismounted cyclist 'crowds' his bike. A labourer, explaining how some pigs had escaped from their stye, pointed to the gate, and said 'Th' old sow, she crod unean it' (pushed underneath it). I remember one day at Lakenham Cricket Ground a fielder let the ball go between his legs to the boundary, and a farmer who was watching said, 'He 'oon't never du to keep pigs.'

A Norfolk boy does not throw a ball: he 'hulls' (hurls) it, or, more gently, he 'cops' (tosses) it to a friend. Bowling, either at cricket or on the bowling-green, is pronounced like bowels.

As might be expected, the Broads and marshlands have their own vocabulary. The old Norfolk trading wherries were propelled, when the wind was contrary, by a 'quant'—a longer, heavier version of a punt pole—which was pushed by a man walking along the narrow 'plankway' (deck). Sailing-yachts are helped along in the same way, but, with the now general use of auxiliary engines, fewer yachtsmen are acquiring the art of quanting over

25

A Swar'ston winder. *See* page 23.

the muddy bottoms of the Norfolk rivers and Broads. Quanting one of the long, low, narrow Norfolk gun punts is a more delicate art: the late Major Anthony Buxton of Horsey says in his book *Travelling Naturalist* (1948) that the waterman who taught him explained, 'Yew kind o' hold the water wi' your feet.'

The beds of reeds and rushes along the banks are called 'ronds', and the boats carry 'rond anchors' for mooring. The woods of alder, willow, and sallow are 'carrs'. The roads across the marshes are 'carnsers' (causeways), and the quays, where in the old days wherries were loaded and unloaded, are 'staithes'. Dikes are alternatively 'deeks' or 'holls'—but a holl may also be a dry ditch on the uplands. Deeks are 'bottomfied', 'fyed out', or 'didled out' with a 'mearger' (long-handled scythe), a 'didle' (long-handled shovel), a 'shore-cutter' (knife), and a 'crome' (rake). Floating islands of reed and weeds are called 'hover'.

A 'roger' is a miniature whirlwind that sweeps across the marshes—yachtsmen are warned to beware of it—and a storm is a 'tempest'.

A 'ligger' is a plank laid across a deek for a bridge. It is also a kind of float—that 'ligs' or lies on the surface of the water—used for pike-fishing. Eelmen, from their old tarred houseboats, lay nets called 'bosoms' and 'pods' across the rivers and dikes. Another method of catching eels used to be to spear them with an eel 'pick' or 'pritch'—a kind of flat-pronged trident that was plunged again and again into the mud in the bottom of the river until the eels were caught between its prongs.

Another kind of pritch was a shepherd's 'fold-pritch'—a heavy iron tool that was used to make holes in which to plant the hurdles that enclosed the sheep, whose dung enriched the soil even as they grazed the stubble after harvest or were fed in winter on turnips. But the shepherd and his 'page' (the boy who helped him) have now disappeared from the Norfolk arable land, along with the old four-course shift of crops which depended heavily on 'the golden hoof' of great flocks of sheep, and it would now be hard to find a fold-pritch outside a museum. It must be nearly a hundred years since West Norfolk shepherds counted their sheep by the primeval:

> *Ina, tina, tether, wether, pink,*
> *Hater, slater, sara, dara, dick.*

The thatcher and his 'toad' (boy) survive because of the demand for the beautiful and durable Norfolk reed thatch for the roofs of country houses, and the Broadland reed-cutters still reap a winter harvest of reed bundled into 'fathoms', which the holiday-makers see piled up on the staithes.

But, thanks to combine-harvesters, there are no more stacks of corn on the Norfolk farms, to be thatched with straw, with the thatcher's toad 'yelming' (combing out) 'gavels' of long, straight straws to carry up the ladder to his master on the roof of the stack. Neither is 'troshing' (threshing) a winter occupation; nor is there home-brewed beer to be carried out in a great 'gotch' (jug) to slake the thirst of the threshing gang. The combine reaps and threshes in one operation; and, after the grain has gone through the mechanical drier into sacks, a plastic tarpaulin is good enough to cover the stacks of baled straw.

There is no more need for boys proudly to take charge of wagons in the harvest fields, and 'haller howdjee' to the horses. There are no more 'shoofs' (sheaves) to be adroitly bound with a bond of twisted straws and set up in 'shocks'; no more reapers to form a circle round a stranger and, taking their time from the leader, 'haller largees'—that is, shout 'largesse', for a tip. No doubt we should be glad to be rid of the poverty that gave rise to such a custom.

Similarly, there are few 'harvest horkeys'—feasts set up by the master and his wife in the barn, that gave the impoverished nineteenth-century farm-workers and their families what was perhaps their only taste in the year of butcher's meat. Such horkeys as survive are conducted in a different fashion—as like as not, in a restaurant. But a scarecrow (when you can find one) is still called a 'mawkin'.

Mechanization has gone so far that farm-horses are now a great rarity, and the plough-man's commands to his horses—'cubbear' to turn them to the left or near side, 'weesh' to turn them to the right, and 'holt' when they had turned enough—are becoming a distant memory. So are the processions of farm- and cart-horses to the great Easter Horse Sale at Tombland Fair on Norwich Hill—their hoofs polished, and their manes and tails 'tricolated' (decorated) with ribbons and plaited straw. As to fairs, King's Lynn has its famous mart that opens on St Valentine's Day; but in the villages a fair used to be a 'gant'—as in Mattishall Gant and Ryburgh Gant.

We still talk of a small paddock as a 'pightle', and of odd corners of land as 'scutes', and the back lanes of villages as 'lokes'. As for the hedges—where they have not been destroyed to make bigger fields it has become deplorably common to mutilate them with mechanical slashers. The hedger's skill with his edge-tools—his 'flasher', his 'bagging-hook', and his 'scrogger'—is rare, and a well-laid hedge is a very uncommon sight in Norfolk today. Barbed-wire is more economical.

However, we still have 'grups' (shallow trenches) cut in the roadside verges to drain rainwater into the ditches. And one good old Norfolk word has served to explain a practice of modern highway engineers:

'What do the Surweyor mean when he say we're got to stagger these hare cross-roads?' inquired a rustic member of the County Council.

The then Chairman (the late Russell Colman, who was an authority on the dialect), answered, 'He means put 'em on the sosh.'

Anything in Norfolk that is askew, or slanting, is 'soshens' or 'on the sosh'. Another good word—used by a workman to explain the broken helve of an axe—is 'spolt', meaning brittle or short-grained. If the helve had split he would have said it was 'sprung'. But spolt, applied to vegetables, can be a term of praise: it means they are crisp and fresh. If they are stale, they are 'clung' or 'foisty'.

I am told that, in Mid-Norfolk, vegetables that have run to seed are said to have 'spolted'—but the more common term for run to seed is 'bolted'.

A consequence of the use of chemical weedkillers and the ploughing out of hedgerows, is that many wild flowers, once common, are getting scarce, and their local names may disappear. Even the red poppy, which inspired the Victorian Clement Scott's poem 'The Garden of Sleep' about the ruined church of Sidestrand, and gave the name 'Poppyland' to the Cromer district, now appears but thinly in the fields of ripening barley and wheat, and the farmers say 'good riddance' to what they call 'corn canker'. They would be just as glad to get rid of 'dindle' (sow thistle). But it seems sad to me that 'pagles' (cowslips) are now more commonly to be seen in railway-cuttings than in meadows.

We are also in danger of losing some of our birds. We have more than enough 'dows' (pigeons)—in a county that nowadays grows an enormous acreage of peas for the canning and freezing plants, pigeons have become a plague. And the ubiquitous sparrows and starlings have been as successful as man himself in adapting themselves to the spread of

'That fare to quackle me.' *See* page 25.

A gotch of beer for the bellringers. *See* page 27.

towns, but we still distinguish 'dunnocks' (hedge-sparrows) from house-sparrows. And we call song-thrushes by the beautiful old name of mavis, or, in the Norfolk tongue, 'mavish', whereas the missel-thrush is known as the 'fulfer'.

The bullfinch (beloved of those who do not suffer its depredations upon the buds of their fruit trees) is the 'blood ulf', the greenfinch is the 'green ulf', and the chaffinch is the 'spink'. Yellow-hammers are 'gulehams' or 'gulers'. The great tit is called a 'black-cap', and the blue tit is a 'pick-cheese', while swifts are 'devilins'.

'Aberdevine' is a strange name for the siskin. It is said to have been coined by London dealers over 200 years ago as a high-sounding name for the siskin as a cage-bird. Similarly the goldfinch, otherwise known by the gallant name of 'King Harry', is also called the 'draw-water'—from the time when goldfinches used to be kept in cages with a little wheel and a chain, with which the bird drew up a little bucket of water for itself.

This is not a pleasant thought nowadays, when we agree with Blake that:

> *A Robin Redbreast in a Cage*
> *Puts all Heaven in a Rage.*

But I know an old lady who remembers, from her childhood at the turn of the century, seeing the Norwich 'snobs' (shoemakers)—who were great bird-fanciers—walk out at week-ends to the meadows of Lakenham, with cages on their backs, to trap linnets and finches. I doubt whether that practice, reprehensible though we now think it, was nearly so destructive of song-birds as mechanized and chemical agriculture.

Fust that friz, then ter snew ... *See* page 33.

IV

THE MANNER OF SPEAKING

Although the vocabulary is weakening, an East Anglian is still marked just as clearly by his distinctive grammar and turn of phrase as he is by his accent. Nowhere else in England do people make so much use of the word 'that', which comes into an East Anglian's speech where anybody else would say 'it' or 'this'. When a borrower returns a book, the owner says, 'Thankee for bringin' that back. The missus was now axin' where that 'ud got to. I'll put that on the shulf.' And the borrower replies, 'I'm right glad you lent that to me. I ought to ha' brung that back suner, oonly that fared as if I cou'nt put that down. Tha's a maaster fine story, that that is.'

But one of the differences between the present and an older generation is that the older generation was more inclined to say 'ter' instead of 'it'. For instance, there is the old Norfolk description of a hard winter, which also illustrates the peculiar East Anglian conjugation of verbs: 'Fust ter friz, then ter snew, then ter thew, an' then that tunned right round an' friz all oover agin.'

Scholars tell me East Anglian grammar is good Anglo-Saxon, and good Old English. Chaucer says of a wealthy yeoman that 'it snewed in his house of meat and drink'.

Similarly, an East Anglian does not tell you he hoed his potatoes; he 'hew his taters' and he 'sew' (not sowed) his peas, he 'swum' (not swam) in the river, he 'rid' (not rode) his bicycle, and he 'gan' or 'gonned' (not gave) his daughter a book of 'gays' (pictures) for her birthday. He also makes a good deal of use of what grammarians call the historic present. He 'see [not saw] you a-comin'—which is a saying that may indicate that he got the better of a bargain. 'I reckon he see yew a-comin' ' is the uncomforting rejoinder to anyone who comes back from market complaining that he has been worsted by a dealer.

We retain—or did until recently—some of the Old English plurals. Children are 'childer', houses are 'housen', and mice are 'meece' or 'meesen'.

Other pleasant bits of Old English are 'backus' (back-house) for scullery, and 'neatus' (neat-house) for cattle-shed. We still talk about 'haysel' for haymaking, but 'barleysel', for the time of sowing barley, is now uncommon. However, country people still have the courteous habit of giving even strangers 'the seal of the day' when they pass them in the road. Speaking of an arrogant squire who did not respond to such a greeting, an old countryman said, 'I made my obedience to him, but he would neither speak nor grunt.' A neighbour observed, with the same quiet and deadly irony which is characteristic of East Anglia, 'He was meant for a gentleman but spoilt in the maaking.'

When we know a man by sight but not by name, we 'know him to see to'. We are sparing of plurals in that we talk of so many 'ton of straw' or so many 'cran of herring', but we make up for it when we add a gratuitous 's' to people's surnames, so that a Mr Hill becomes Mr Hills, or a Mrs Field becomes Mrs Fields. When we invite friends to our houses we say, 'Come yew up to mine', or 'Come yew round to ours.' Notice the 'come you', which may also be 'Go yew round to mine', or 'Do yew come an' see me', or 'Fetch yew them taters.'

It is Biblical English—'Go ye into the village over against you.' We in Norfolk use it constantly.

And when the guests, having been round to 'ours', are going back to 'theirs', we do not say 'Good-bye' we say 'Farewell', or just as likely, 'Fare ye well, together.' 'Together' is another of our favourite words. A man drinking the health of the company will say, 'Here's my opinion of you, together.' Or a mother, calling a laggard child, will exclaim, 'Come yew on, together, an' stop puttin' on your parts.' Even when we are addressing only one other person, it is still 'together'.

Which was once a great embarrassment to a highly respectable and virtuous London girl, when for the first time she spent a week-end at the home of her Norfolk fiancé. His parents made her very welcome, and she slept soundly in a pretty little bedroom on the far side of the house from the young man. Imagine her astonishment when, on coming down to breakfast the following morning, she was greeted by her prospective father-in-law (a chapel deacon) with: 'Well, my dear, did ye sleep well, together?'

'Now' is another of our pet words in Norfolk. We do not say 'I'm just coming', but 'I'm now a-comin'.' Or a housewife will say, 'I'm now a-puttin' the dinner on', or 'Come yew in out o' the garden, George, yar supper is now riddy.' To which George will reply from the 'backus', 'Hold yew hard, me ole bu'y, I'm now a-taakin' o' my butes orf.'

'Well, I never did, in all my born days!'—often shortened to 'Well, I never!'—is our expression of astonishment, while the description 'master' conveys admiration. Thus a man might say, 'Tha's a maaster great stack as Giles ha' got on the twenty-acre.' To which his friend, having looked at the stack, might reply, 'Well, I never! Tha's a soler, that is, ent it?' This conversation might go on while they were sitting under the lee of a hedge, eating their 'elevenses', with a 'thumb bit', consisting of as much bread and cheese and onion as may conveniently be held between the thumb and fingers of the left hand, and sliced and conveyed to the mouth with a 'shut-knife' held in the right hand. An afternoon snack is 'beaver'.

There are many other words and phrases that mark us as Norfolk, wherever we are in the world. For instance, I was once walking with a friend in Sussex when it came on to rain. I made for a clump of trees, and said, 'Come on, let's stand up out of the rain.' My friend looked at me in astonishment. Nowhere except in East Anglia do people 'stand up out of the rain'.

But most extraordinary of all are our multiple uses of the word 'do'—or, as we pronounce it, 'dew' or 'du'. Not only does it serve all the common purposes of the verb 'to do', in East Anglia it can also mean 'if', 'but', 'although', or 'if not'. Oddly enough, dew on the grass is 'dag'. Mr Anthony Hamond, of Ingham, once wrote an imaginary monologue illustrating every possible Norfolk use of 'dew'. The scene is a country railway station, where a mother is seeing her small boy off on a holiday with his uncle. She says:

Dew yew make him dew as yew dew: don't, he 'on't dew as he should dew. If he don't dew as he should dew, I should give him a dewin' tew if I was yew. We dew our tew. I always say tew'm, 'Don't dew it, don't dew it, 'cause if yew dew that don't dew'; and neither dew it, dew it? So dew yew mind what he dew dew. I don't want he should go and dew anything like he done up at Mrs Dewin's, Tuesday. Mrs Dunne come out time he was a-dewin' of it, and when she see what he done to Mrs Dewin's dewins she say, 'Oh! Whatever have yew done?' she say, and runned off to fetch Mrs Dewin'. That wouldn't ha' done, Mrs Dewin' say, for Mrs Dunne to a' done nothin' tew the boy, dew I might ha' gone round,

'Dew yew make him dew as yew dew.   *See* page 34.

Rafty old weather. *See* page 39.

she say, and got aboard o' Mrs Dunne for nothin', not knowin', but Oh! what a t'dew when Mr Dewin' come back an' see Mrs Dunne gettin' all the dewins. 'Hew done it?' he says. 'Why, little Alfie,' Mrs Dunne say, so he say, 'Dew yew tell his mother from me, if he dew'ny more like that I'll dew him!' Old lady Dunne see him tew, but she was then arter some feathers for old deaffie Gotobed, and y'know what an old dardalum-dew he is, so that put har in a stew for a minute for fear the wind blew. Well, that was a how-d'ye-dew, I tell yer, and Mrs Dewin' then got all ready for Dunham's man to take 'em. Mrs Dunne say little Dewin' wouldn't never ha' done half what he done, but there y'are. Well, there y'go. Fare y'well.'

Believe it or not, a Norfolk woman can read this aloud, very fast, and there is nothing at all strange about it to East Anglian ears. It sounds for all the world like one of our village gossips, hard at it.

Mr Hamond has also introduced our characteristic use of the double negative. In East Anglia we seldom say 'no' once: we say it twice or even three times to give it proper emphasis. Thus, a postman to a child that has run to the garden gate to fetch the letters: 'Noo, my dear, that ent a mite o' use yew runnin' arter me. I ain't got naathin' for noobra [nobody], not today I hent.'

Our gossips 'go on and on, like a pig in a harvest field'. They are not to be trusted with confidences because 'a dog what fetch 'll carry'. One of them said, after a hasty wedding, followed very soon by a baptism, 'The little old boy, he come just in time for a slice o' the weddin' caake.' If a marriage turned out unfortunately, they would say of the hapless bride, 'She'll suck sorrow by pailfuls.' Or if it were the husband who was the injured party, 'He're swallered shaame and drank arter it.'

The rural philosophers have a tolerant saying for a talkative woman who is nevertheless a good housewife: 'A hen what dorn't prate 'oon't lay.' But a rude man was 'brought up on the end of a hog-line'. He might be reminded that 'yew'll catch more flies wi' a spuneful o' honey than a gallon o' winegar'.

A fool has 'no more sense than a May gosling', or 'he dorn't know great A from the gable end'. There is a half-contemptuous, half-compassionate description of a village idiot: 'He want gitten' [begetting] oover again.' It might have been the poor idiot who, having been roundly abused, complained, 'He called me from a pig to a dog.' But a man who is merely stupid is 'as wooden as a pump' or 'as thick as a hedge'.

I am surprised to be told that the expression 'meat for manners' (referring to an employee who got board and lodging but no wages) is peculiar to Norfolk.

The Norfolk use of metaphor is vivid and often wounding. It is particularly unwise, in this county, to hold forth on a subject of which you know nothing, because if your audience do not tell you to your face that you are 'talking squit', they will remark as soon as you have gone that 'He dorn't know no more about that than a crow do about a Sunday.' Neither must you thrust yourself too hurriedly into Norfolk affairs, or you will be 'too eager, like Farmer Cubitt's calf as trotted t'ree mile to suck a bull'. In the same vein is the saying about an unsuccessful candidate for the village choir: 'He ent got no more ear for music than Balls's bull as dossed the fiddler oover the fence.'

If you are inquisitive, the answer will be 'What d'yew want to know that for?' If you persist, you will be told bluntly, 'I aren't a-gorn to tell yew all my know.' The answer to a tactless remark is, 'I'll take it from whence it come, as the booy say when the dickey [donkey] kicked him.' After that, the conversation will be 'short and sweet, like a dickey's gallop'.

37

Caught in her dissables. *See* page 39.

But an honest man is 'up an' down straight, like a yard o' pump water'. A thin man is 'like two boards clapped together'. An overgrown boy is 'run up o' legs'. An ailing child 'pingles' with its food, and 'dorn't eat noo more'n a hen's noseful'.

A big, blowsy woman or girl is 'a slummockin' great mawther'. If she is also untidy 'she look as if she're been dragged t'ru a bush faggot'. If she is aggressive and cheeky she is 'silly-bold'. If she puts on an affected voice or manner, she is 'primmicking' or 'framing'.

But a pompous little man is 'a botty little man'. If he is talkative, he is a 'spuffler'. It may also be that, in his self-importance, 'he hah an' hacker in his talk'—although 'hukker' also means stutter. If he is bald, he has 'a head like a bladder o' lard'.

A lazy man is 'as idle as Hall's dog, what died 'cause that was tew laazy to eat'. Thrifty people are commended with 'some eat their brown bread first and white arterwards'. A man who does not live up to his religious professions is 'Sunday saint, weekday devil', 'His religion is copyhold and he haven't taken it up', and 'His conscience is made of stretching leather.' Resentment of tithe-paying is epitomized in the saying, 'As big as the parson's barn.'

Our Norfolk equivalent of 'Penny wise and pound foolish' is 'Spare at the spigot and waste at the bung hole.' Instead of 'Neither fish, fowl nor good red herring', we say, 'Neither he, she, nor yit the old woman.' 'Make do and mend' is 'If that 'oon't puddin' that'll froise.' (If it won't make pudding it'll fry.)

An old lady who was feeling her years said, 'I reckon I shall ha' to goo to Bungay an' git new-bottomed'—which was a reference to a time when the little town of Bungay, in the Waveney Valley, was a centre of the leather trade, and leather breeches were taken there to be mended. When talking of colours, we say newly washed sheets are 'as white as white', or a child's unwashed hands are 'as black as black'. A person with grey hair is 'as grey as a dow [dove].'

As to weather, when a 'tempest' (thunderstorm) is coming up, we say 'That's dark over Will's mother's.' When the storm breaks we say 'That's teeming with rain.' But a drizzle is a 'smur of rain' or a 'mizzle of rain'. A damp day is 'a daggly old day' and a mist is a 'roke'. Wet, windy weather is 'rafty old weather'.

When we ask the time we say, 'What's the clock?' The answer may be 'Tha's half arter five,' or 'That want a quarter to six.' 'Ah!' says the inquirer, 'But accordin-lie to the clock, that ha' gone six a'riddy.' 'Dorn't yew pay noo regard to that clock,' replies the householder, 'That git.' That is to say, the clock gains.

We say 'that dorn't signify' when we mean it doesn't matter. 'Accordingly'—pronounced 'accordin-lie'—is one of our favourite long words. Another is 'imitate', but in the Norfolk tongue it means 'attempt'; for instance, 'I shou'nt imitate to du that if I was yew.' We are also fond of 'regard', but usually in a negative sense: 'Yew dorn't want to pay noo regard to him—he dorn't know B from a bull's foot.' 'Jurisdiction' is another one: a youth, asked about some matter of business in his father's workshop, might reply, 'Yew'll ha' to wait till my father come. Y'see, he have the jurisdiction of that.' And how did the fashionable word *deshabille* find its way into common use in Norfolk villages—as when a woman, if the Vicar is tactless enough to call on a Monday washing-day, apologizes for being 'in her dissables'?

Main roads in East Anglia are still 'turnpikes': 'Keep yew a-gorn till yew come tew a barnd on your roight. A' the yon side o' the barnd the rood fork to your left, an' there's a sign-poost what say, "To Garveston". Now dorn't yew pay noo regard to that. Yew want

Tricolating up a shed. *See* page 41.

to just keep on a-bearin' to your roight until yew come to the tu'npike. That ent more'n a matter o' t'ree moile.'

'Tricolate' is one of our own inventions. It can mean 'decorate', but more commonly it means 'patch up'. When a man has repaired his garden 'shud' (shed) and put new roofing-felt on the roof, his neighbour will say, 'I reckon yew're tricolated that up a treat, bor.'

People have to 'summer and winter' a newcomer before he is accepted in a Norfolk village—some say this is a process that takes anything up to twenty years. Anyone from outside the charmed circle of East Anglia is either a Londoner or 'come from the Sheers [Shires]'. In any event, 'he come from away', and must be treated with due caution. 'If he dorn't like it he can lump it.' He has, poor fellow, to learn the language in a county where, if the children fidget, they 'jiffle', and if they get excited they 'go shanny'. But the children will learn more quickly than their parents; they will soon become bilingual, and go to the village shop for a bag of 'cushies' (sweets). In the shop they may meet an old lady who still calls her shopping-bag a 'poke', and her tabby cat a 'Cyprus cat'. They will fish in the beck for 'poddle-ladles' (tadpoles) and 'stannicles' (sticklebacks). At the sea-side they will gather 'pinpanches' (winkles) from the hummocks of flint exposed at low tide, and bathe in the 'lows' between the sandbanks. On the marshes they will hear the redshank 'sharming'.

Or am I drawing too fanciful a picture of villages which are fast becoming suburban? As we also say in Norfolk, 'Then was then and now is now.'

V

NORFOLK PLACES

Norfolk place-names and their pronunciation baffle the uninitiated. It is well known that Norwich rhymes with 'porridge', but who could guess that Wymondham is 'Windum', Costessey is 'Cossey', Alburgh is 'Arburgh', Raveningham is 'Ranningham', Acle is 'Aycle' and not 'Ackle' or 'Ackley', and Cley is 'Cly' (although telephone-operators nowadays call it 'Clay')? 'Hulver', the pretty old dialect word for holly, gives its name to a Suffolk village near Beccles.

Although the once-great East Coast herring fishery is now, alas, defunct, Yarmouth people are still called 'bloaters'. Cromer people are 'Cromer crabs', but for no reason that anyone can explain the inhabitants of Sheringham, which also has its crab and lobster fishery, are called 'shannocks' (from the dialect word 'shanny', meaning wild or excited). On the other hand, an old rhyme says:

> *Cromer crabs, Runton dabs,*
> *Beeston babies, Sheringham ladies,*
> *Weybourne witches, Salthouse ditches.*
> *And the Blakeney people*
> *Stand on the steeple*
> *And crack hazel-nuts*
> *With a five-farthing beetle [mallet].*

Farther along the coast we have:

> *Blakeney bulldogs,*
> *Morston dodmen [snails],*
> *Binham bulls,*
> *Stewkey [Stiffkey] trolls,*
> *Wells bitefingers.*

'Wells bitefingers' is an allusion to an injurious story that Wells people used to lure ships on to the treacherous sands off the North Norfolk coast, and bite off the fingers of drowned sailors in order to get at their rings.

A kinder jingle about another group of coastal villages simply says:

> *Gimingham, Trimingham,*
> *Knapton and Trunch,*
> *Northrepps and Southrepps*
> *Lie all in a bunch.*

In what seems to be a cryptic reference to the medieval riches of the now-silted North Norfolk ports, another old rhyme says:

> *London, York and Coventry,*
> *And seven Burnhams by the sea.*

These are Burnham Market, Burnham Westgate, Burnham Thorpe (Nelson's birthplace), Burnham Norton, Burnham Sutton, Burnham Deepdale, and Burnham Overy. Indeed, since Burnham Overy is in fact two villages—one called Overy Town and the other Overy Staithe—you can if you like make it eight Burnhams. At any rate, the old rhymer said no harm of them, but who made up this savage rhyme about a baker's dozen of pleasant Broadland villages?

> *Parnser [Panxworth] dogs and Bastwick [Woodbastwick] bitches,*
> *Ranworth coots and Walsham witches.*
> *Upton church without a steeple—*
> *Dirty roads and wicked people.*
> *Acle asses, Moulton mules,*
> *Beighton bears and Freethorpe fules [fools],*
> *Halvergate hares and Reedham rats,*
> *Southwood swine and Cantley cats.*

After this piece of rustic invective one can no longer be shocked by the mixed Norfolk and Suffolk:

> *Pakefield for poverty,*
> *Lowestoft for poor.*
> *Gorleston for pretty girls,*
> *Yarmouth for whores.*
> *Caister for waterdogs,*
> *California for pluck.*
> *Damn and bugger old Winterton—*
> *How black she do look!*

California, by the way, is the name of what is now a bungalow settlement just north of Caister-on-Sea. It is so called because of a find by 'pawkers' (Norfolk for beachcombers) in the latter part of the nineteenth century of a hoard of gold coins. They were of various reigns from Henry VIII to Charles I. A well-known archaeologist, the late Charles Green, thought they must have been buried during the Civil War in a now-forgotten hamlet that was destroyed by coastal erosion: the hoard being exposed again, and scattered in the sand, by another scour of the tides 200 years later. At any rate, one of the 'pawkers'—a Scratby fisherman—found as many as ninety coins, and bought himself a new boat with the proceeds.

43

That dorn't come noo more'n half-way up our maaster's ducks. *See* page 45.

VI

NORFOLK STORIES

A book like this is supposed to contain some Norfolk stories, but I do not care for stock-brokers' stories translated into the dialect and then called Norfolk. I prefer those that seem to have grown out of our local characteristics, one of which is a strong dislike of arrogance. Hence the tale, derived from the early days of motoring, of a 'foreigner' who came upon a ford at the bottom of a rutted lane, and said very haughtily to a rustic who was standing on the footbridge:

'My man, do you think I can drive through here?'

'Why yis,' said the man, 'I reckon yew can drive in all right.'

So the motorist drove in, only to find himself, in midstream, with the water half-way up the bonnet.

'What the devil do you mean,' he shouted angrily, 'by telling me this was fit for motors? You must be an idiot.'

'Well,' said the rustic coolly, 'I dorn't know naathin' about mootor cars, but that dorn't come noo more'n half-way up our maaster's ducks.'

Then, having struck a bargain with the helpless motorist, he trudged away to fetch a horse and a rope, and as he went he muttered to himself with a grin, 'That was right what I towd him about drivin' in, but I di'nt say naathin' about drivin' out agin.'

A similar story concerns a motorist who got lost in what was in those days a maze of lanes between Holt and Cromer. He stopped, and saw a ploughman half-way across a field.

'George,' he shouted, 'Hi, George, can you tell me the way to Cromer?'

The ploughman took not the slightest notice. The motorist kept on shouting, and the man kept on ploughing, until he had reached the headland, turned his horses and stopped them, and then, very slowly, he walked over to the hedge and said:

'What du yew want?'

'I want to know the way to Cromer, George,' said the motorist impatiently.

'Oh,' said the ploughman—then, 'Hew towd yew my naame was George?'

'Well,' said the motorist awkwardly, 'I kind of guessed it.'

'Then yew can blooda well guess the way to Croomer,' replied the ploughman, and, with a 'gurrup' to his horses, resumed his progress across the field.

Both of these stories illustrate the sly Norfolk way of 'laying for' a stranger who thinks he is smarter than the yokels, and letting him make a fool of himself.

There is another such story of a young under-keeper at a pheasant shoot, who was told to look after an important guest from the City, who was a terribly bad shot. The guest blazed away all day, sometimes to the considerable danger of the neighbouring guns, their dogs, or the beaters, but without hitting so much as the tail-feather of a bird. At the end

Fifta-fifta pies. *See* page 47.

of the last drive a terrified little rabbit, caught between the advancing beaters and the line of guns, crouched in a furrow only about ten yards from the City man, who fired the first barrel almost without bringing his gun to his shoulder. The rabbit was, of course, unharmed, and the young keeper, unable by this time to conceal his disgust, exclaimed, 'Shoot 'um again, sir. He di'nt hear ye the first time.'

Concerning rabbits, the late Mr Russell Colman, who was a great teller of Norfolk stories, had a favourite one about the days before myxomatosis, when rabbits were a staple item of commerce in Breckland. A baker in Thetford had such a reputation for his rabbit-pies that he was getting large orders for them from the Norwich shops. One day a close friend of his complained:

'Jack, I can't maake out what ha' come oover them rabbit-pies o' yours. They dorn't fare so taasty as what they used to.'
The baker said confidentially, 'Well, y'see Jimma, tha's all a question o' what tha' Government call supply an' demand. The fac' o' the matter is, I can't git rabbits enow for all o' my customers.'
'So what are yew a-duin' on?' asked Jimmy.
'Bor,' replied the baker in a whisper, 'Atween yew an' me an' the gaatepost, I're had to fill out them pies wi' a mite o' hoss meat.'
'Blast!' said Jimmy, 'How much hoss meat d'yew reckon to put in?'
' 'Bout fifta-fifta,' whispered the baker, with a grin.
'What d'yew mean by fifta-fifta?' asked Jimmy, suspiciously.
'Oh! One hoss, one rabbit,' said the baker.

There is sometimes a touch of humorous exaggeration, akin to the American, in Norfolk stories, but generally we are given to under-statement, like the man who, having been, along with 30,000 other people, to a football cup-tie at Norwich, was asked when he got home whether there was a big crowd—'Well bor,' he said, 'there was several there.'
There is also a nice touch of irony, as with the village carpenter who, while working in a doctor's house, was caught putting putty in his joints to make them fit.

The doctor said, 'I suppose a lump or two of putty has covered up several of your mistakes, George.'
'Yis, doctor,' said George, 'an' I reckon a flag [turf] or tew of grass have covered up several o' your mistakes an' all.'

But for some reason—perhaps the Nonconformist streak in us—we tell more stories against parsons than doctors. For instance, there was the young woman who went to the verger of a village church and asked:

'Kin the reverent christen my little 'un a' Sunday?'
'Noo, my dear, that he can't,' said the verger, 'an' wha's more, that ent a mite o' use yew talkin' about any day afore next Tuesday, 'cause he's a-gorn pike-fishin' a' Monday, an' he're got the font full o' livebait.'

Another parson, less habituated to country life, was delighted, when he came from the city to a rural parish, to find a beautifully kept churchyard, well mown, and with roses blooming beside the path to the church door.

47

'Kin the reverent christen my little 'un a' Sunday?'   *See* page 47.

'Is it not marvellous,' he exclaimed, 'what beauty God can create in his acre?'

'Tha's all very well, sir,' replied the verger, affronted, 'but yew oughter seen what that was like afore I come, an' th'Almighty had it on his own.'

The same parson, on another occasion, was surprised to meet in a narrow lane one of his smallest Sunday school children, driving a large cow. Shrinking nervously into the hedge, he said:

'Good morning, Mary. May I ask where you are going with that enormous animal?'

'Please, sir,' replied Mary, 'I'm a-taakin' old Buttercup to be bulled.'

'Dear me!' said the parson, very shocked, 'But couldn't your father do that?'

'Ooh, no sir!' said Mary, equally shocked, 'That must be a bull.'

Our religion, in Norfolk, is qualified by considerations that are of the earth, earthy. The late Major Anthony Buxton, of Horsey, used to tell a tale of his uncle, the Reverend Charlie Digby, visiting a pious old widow at Warham. Since every man may spell Norfolk as he pleases, and Major Buxton had his own way of suggesting the Norfolk intonation, I give the old lady's story exactly as he wrote it in his book *Travelling Naturalist*:

'Ooh, Mr Digby, Oi had sech a wonderful dream last noight. Moi oold man, he com and set by moi bedsoide and he looked so lovely: he weere such bewtiful clothes and he say such bewtiful weerds. Now, Mr Digby, what d'yew think? They tell me that's a soign o' rain.'

Norfolk people, as Major Buxton observed, have a way of lifting a story to the heights, and then dropping the hearer flatly to earth again. They gulp down enthusiasm as it rises, and here is another Anthony Buxton story to illustrate this point. The speaker is a village gossip:

'He h'ard as how his young woman had took to walkin' along of another young man, an' he said, as he'd *ivry roight* to duu, "You're a slippery slink, yuu are." She took that tarrible to heart, an' she went hoome an' took half a point o' pig wash an' tuu point o' walnut pickle, an' mixed 'em op, an' dronk it down. In the noight she were took o' tarrible pains o' heer insoide, an' she sent for the doctor an' he come an' done all his possibles, but he said as how there was a kind of a seediment o' heer insoide as he couldn't roightly git behoind. An' in the noight she passed away butiful peaceful, loike a socked laazenge'.

In the same vein is the lamentation of the old lady who said:

'Yis, my pore man he fared to git worser an' worserer wi' the misery o' his insoide, until in the end on it the doctor he sent for tha amberlance an' they took him away to tha horspital: but du yew know, I reckon if that hent been for that there poost mortum he'd still ha' been aloive an' with us today.'

A widower, who for thirty years had lived a cat and dog life with a scolding wife, was more easily consoled. Only a month after his wife's funeral he was observed to be 'walking out' with 'a slummocking great mawther' only half his age. One of his friends said:

'Yew want to look out, George. Yew remember what ole Martha used to say, toime she were aloive. She say, "Supposin' I was to goo first, an' George was to marry someone else, I'd scrat my way out o' the graave an' haunt 'um."'

'Ah!' said George, 'But I thowt o' that afore I started courtin' this here young mawther o' mine. Y'see, ole Billa Woods, tha undertaaker, he's a pal o' mine, an' I got him to bury

A-taakin' old Buttercup to be bulled. *See* page 49.

ole Martha faace down'ards, so the harder she scrat, bor, the deeper she'll fare to goo down.'

Equally strong-minded was an old man at Wymondham, of whom this tale is told:

'This ole feller, wot worked on a faarm at Dykebeck, use ter taake a short cut t'ru the cha'chyard. Tha other chaps, they towd him he'd be a-seein' a ghoost, but he oonly laugh at 'em, an' he still kep' a-comin', foive o'clock o' tha mornin', summer an' winter.
'One on 'em thowt he'd play a trick on tha' ole feller, so one mornin' when he heerd him a-comin'—that was December, an' as dark as black hogs—he bopped up from ahind a tombstone an' started a-scrabblin' away wi' his hands and sharmin', "Lemme git back, lemme git back!"
'Tha ole man up wi' his stick an' cracked him acrorst the skull, an' say, "Taake that, yew silly ole bugger, yew shou'nt ha' got out!" '

To pass from inland to the coast, the late Mr Russell Colman, when he was made High Steward of Great Yarmouth, told a story of two Yarmouth skippers of fishing-smacks, who were deputed to present a model of a mission smack to Queen Victoria on behalf of the Mission to Deep Sea Fishermen. This was the leading delegate's report to a meeting of his mates on his return:

'We went up to Buckin'ham Palace an' took that there model, and when we got there, there was a feller met us dressed such as yew never saw, an' he say to us, "Hev yew got that there model for the Queen, together?"
'I say to him, "Yis, that we hev," I say.
'So he say to me, "Come yew along o' me then."
'Well, bor, we went t'ru rume arter rume, an' at the finish we come to a funny great curtain, an' he say, "Stand yew here, an' when this here curtain is drawed to one side, du yew go in," he say.
'Well, if yew believe me, I'd looked over that model an' went on lookin' over it a score times, an' I hadn't never seen naathin' wrong with it. Then the curtain drawed to one side, an' there set the Queen, an' we maade our obedience to har, an' I walked up, a-holdin' of that there model.
'An' just afore I gan that to har I looked down, an' blow me if the peak halyards worn't fast on the port side!'
'Whatever did the Queen say to that lot?' asked one of the fishermen, aghast at such an error.
'The Queen,' replied the old skipper, 'behaaved like a perfect laady. She didn't pay noo regard.'

Coming to modern times, a new crop of stories is growing up about the relations of rural Norfolk with the executives of the managerial revolution that is taking place in Norwich. For instance, a rising young executive and his wife had renovated, at great expense—and with a pair of (electric) coach lamps on either side of the front door—the Old Rectory, Oaking-ham. They were fortunate enough to inherit the old pensioner who had looked after the garden for the previous occupant. But, having entered into their new residence—with

'A line an' a rule guide many a fule.' *See* page 53.

horse-brasses above the carefully restored open fireplace—they visited a garden centre, and spent the next week-end making a new plan for the garden. The executive took it to his office and got a draughtsman to draw it up as a blue print, with the shrubbery, the rockery, the herbaceous borders, and the rose garden all exactly placed and measured.

Next morning his wife proudly took the plan out to the potting-shed and explained it to the old gardener, who did not approve of it, but decided, since he wanted to keep his job, that he had better be tactful:

'Ah, ma'am!' he said, 'Tha's a maaster fine plan what your husband ha' drawed. We hent never had naathin' like that afore. Y'see, ole Canon Chasuble, he used to leave that to me to put the plants in where I knew they would grow the best: pore ole gentleman, how he loved his rooses unean his study winder, where yew want to put that there heather garden! All the saame, I reckon this here plan's a maasterpiece. I can see I shall ha' to git a line on to that there. 'Cause yew know what they say, dorn't ye, ma'am? "A line an' a rule guide many a fule." '

Another story describes an executive driving his 'Jag' along one of those deceptive Norfolk country roads which, after running for a mile or more as straight as if they had been drawn with a ruler, suddenly make a right-angled bend. The road was empty, the Jaguar was doing well over seventy, and the executive was thinking what he was going to tell his friends at the golf club, when all of a sudden he came to the bend. And just in the middle of the bend was a field gate, and out of the gateway came a tractor, drawing a trailer laden with about five tons of sugar-beet.

The executive, with great presence of mind, managed to skid round the rear of the trailer and shoot through the gateway into the field, where his car, after turning two somersaults, finished upside down in the middle of the field. The tractor-driver, turning to his mate who was riding on the trailer, remarked, 'Blast, bor! Tha's a good job we come out o' that there field, du he'd a' had us.'

Finally, here is a story told by the late Mr B. Knyvet Wilson in his book *Norfolk Tales and Memories* (1930) about the reputation of East Anglians for being suspicious of strangers. He heard it from a Suffolk man, who reckoned the suspicion was all on the Norfolk side—although this may have been the pot calling the kettle black. The Suffolk man was of the sort that used to be called a 'dickey-dealer' or a 'higgler': that is, one who drove about in a ramshackle cart, dealing in donkeys, ponies, hens, pigs, calves, furniture, farm implements, or whatever came his way. At the time of the story, which was the early 1920s, he had risen to an ancient Ford van, and lived at Wymondham in Norfolk. What he told Knyvet Wilson was this:

'Well, Mr Wilson, the t'other day I'd been oover to Bury market, an' I'd had a long day. I wanted to come hoome when that was wery late indeed, an' that was wery foggy. (It often is after market days.) An' when I come in my little ole mootor to Winfarthin'—well, there I lorst my way. Now, Mr Wilson, yew know how all them there roods near Winfarthin' goo a criss-crossin' about! At last I see a little old cottage on the roodside, an' I went an' hammered on the door.

'Arter a wery long time someone lit a candle in one of them little bedrooms in the roof like, an' a funny little ole feller put his hid out o' tha winder—he was in his nightshu't.

' "Hullo!" he say.

' "Hullo, yerself!" I say, an' I towd him I was right sorry to distarb him that time o' night, but I'd lorst my rood an' I wanted to git to Wymondham.

' "Oh," he say, "Wymondham?" he say.

' "Yis," I say, "Wymondham".

' "Ah!" he say, "Now which way did yew *come*?"

' "Well," I say, "now that dorn't matters which way I come, dew it?", I say.

' "Noo," he say. . . . An' then he say, "Well, which way *did* yew come?"

'Well then, Mr Wilson, I lorst my temper—that I did. I was wholly riled, an' I say to him, I say, "What the devil du that matters to yew which way I *come*?" I say. "Du yew put me on my rood to Wymondham, an' I can git on an' yew can git back to bed!"

'An' then he say, "Noo, that dorn't matters to me which way yew *come*, noo more that dorn't matters to me which way yew *goo*!"

' "Good night!" he say, an du yew know, Mr Wilson, he put his hid in an' shet the winder.'

A slummockin' great mawther. *See* page 39.

VII

CAN BROAD NORFOLK SURVIVE?

In the Introduction to his monumental *English Dialect Grammar* and *English Dialect Dictionary*, which were published in 1905, Dr Joseph Wright said: 'There can be no doubt that pure dialect speech is rapidly disappearing even in country districts, owing to the spread of information and to modern facilities for intercommunication. The writing of this grammar was begun none too soon, for, had it been delayed another twenty years, I believe it would then be quite impossible to get together sufficient pure dialect material to enable anyone to give a mere outline of the phonology of our dialects as they existed at the close of the nineteenth century.'

I suppose the fact that Broad Norfolk has lasted so long is due to the unkind truth—true right down to the 1920s—of the saying that 'Norfolk is cut off to the north and east by the sea, and to the south and west by the London and North Eastern Railway.' It is only now that the combined influences of motor transport, electrification, North Sea gas, London overspill, television, and air travel are drawing us into the main stream.

It is nevertheless remarkable that the language of the North Folk, the South Folk, and the East Saxons, whose ancestors settled 1,500 years ago between the North Sea and the then undrained Fens, has survived until the 1970s with a different intonation and accent, a different turn of phrase, and to some considerable extent a different vocabulary and grammar, from those of any other part of Britain. It has been observed that it bears some resemblance to the speech of New England; many of the Pilgrim Fathers (including the forefathers of Abraham Lincoln) came from East Anglia, and traces of their dialect—as well as the names of many Norfolk and Suffolk towns and villages—are still to be found along the north-eastern seaboard of the United States.

Yet, even under the Saxon Heptarchy, the Kingdom of East Anglia was but a minor one, subject to the stronger Midland Kingdom of Mercia, before it was overrun by the invading Danes. The dialect of the common folk, it seems, is stronger and more persistent than changes of government; and stronger than invaders, elements of whose languages it absorbs into itself. It remains to be seen whether it can survive industrialization, at a time when our villages are becoming suburban and our very agriculture is turning into 'agro-industry'.

I do not suppose East Anglian has ever been spoken by much more than a million people. It has never had a poet to glorify it, as Burns did Lowland Scots, in immortal poetry. Indeed, it has scarcely had even a minor poet like Barnes, of Dorset, to make use of the sounds and cadences of the dialect. The best Norfolk poets I have known have been humble versifiers, like the late C. L. (Charlie) Clark, who was a country blacksmith before he sat on the Labour side of Norwich City Council. Poets in local government are scarcer than linnets within the Arctic Circle, so verses like Clark's 'The Team-man's Lament', which never got further than the local paper, are things to treasure. I found this in a newspaper cutting of 1947:

I arnt agin tractors. Not at all.
They du git over some ground.
No doubt we want more on 'em.
But I du miss my hosses.

You carn't call a tractor good company.
Will that hear ye come inter the yard
An' let ye know tha's pleased to see ye?
That ha' got lugs med o' steel
But du they tahn backards to listen
Ter ivery wahd you say to 'em?
No fear they don't, not them.

That earnt no good sayin' 'Woosh'
Nor yit 'Cubbear' to a tractor.
That hearnt got a nice sorft nose
Like welvet
What snubble up agin yer pocket
Fer a napple or a bit o' sweet.

Why, a hoss is werry near a Christian.
That know Sunday from week-day.
Go you inter the yard a Sunday mornin',
You'll find 'em all layin' down.
They know werry well thass Sunday.

D'you remember them two brown 'uns?
Prince and Captain we naamed 'em.
I was there when they were born,
Exactly a twelvemonth atwin 'em.
I browt 'em up, I brook 'em in
By the side o' thar old mother.

Ah, they wor a pair o' hosses,
The best round here for miles,
Lovely ringles all over thar coats,
Dapples our old man useter call 'em.
Thar coats were like a bit o' silk.

You carn't curry-comb a tractor
Nor yit you carn't coox it.
If you du that'll bahn yer hand
Or else freeze it.

Ah, tractors are all werry well.
They wholly git over some ground.
No doubt we want more on 'em,
But still thass a masterpiece
How much I miss my hosses.

Yew carn't call a tractor good company / Will that hear ye come inter the yard.   *See* page 57.

This is true sentiment even if it is not great poetry. It is also very good Norfolk: the best I have found in my research for this book. For it comes from a man who spoke Norfolk as his native language, and wrote it from his heart.

But to return to the question of the survival of the dialect, it has never been worth any actor's while to learn East Anglian—not enough people outside the province understand it. One modern dramatist, Arnold Wesker, who must have a very good ear, made telling use of Norfolk in his *Roots* (which was, however, a city man's protest against the narrowness and crudity of village life as he saw it through the eyes of his heroine). I dare to say that *Roots* got its best performance at the Maddermarket Theatre in Norwich, which was able to enlist Norfolk actors to play it.

For the rest, professional actors not unnaturally find Mummerset is good enough for any play in a rural setting—their biggest audiences are in the big cities. Similarly, generations of comedians have made reputations as Cockney, Scots, or Lancashire comedians, but nobody is going to find fame or fortune as a Norfolk or Suffolk comedian—although the late Sidney Grapes (the Boy John) had a very good time as a gifted amateur in his own province, and also made some impression on the Midland Region of the B.B.C. More recently the Singing Postman, with his modern Norfolk ballads, has more than once appeared in the top half of the charts of popular records, but he, again, is a rare bird.

Sidney Grapes's 'Boy John' letters on the humours of village life, written between 1946 and 1958, will be loved as long as there are any surviving copies of the two booklets in which they were collected after his death. They are the genuine article, written by a man who lived all his life in a Broadland village, spoke the dialect as he had heard it from his parents, and spelt it as he pleased. I must also mention my colleague, Maurice Woods, London editor of the *Eastern Daily Press*, who, most remarkably, has kept up 'Harbert's News from Dumpton' in the *Norwich Mercury* for more than twenty years after his departure from his native county. But, in general, what has been written in Norfolk or Suffolk dialect is inclined to suffer from having been written *de haut en bas*, by the squire who liked to chuckle over it, the parson who found it etymologically interesting, or the doctor who found it quaint. The people who spoke it as their mother tongue seldom wrote it, because they were unconscious of speaking it, and, when they had occasion to write at all, wrote in the standard English of their time: when East Anglian words and phrases slipped in, it was by accident rather than by design.

East Anglian dialect has survived, above all, by an oral tradition. Tape recordings, which are now being made of it, have come late in the day. For I am convinced that Joseph Wright was a true prophet when he said that so long ago as 1905 pure dialect speech was rapidly disappearing. The dialect that even old country-folk speak today is not, I am afraid, quite the same language as their grandparents spoke. The outside influences, since then, have been too numerous and powerful to leave Broad Norfolk or any other dialect unchanged.

The numerous 'foreigners' from London and the Shires, who have come of recent years to live and work among us, are much interested in the strange dialect they hear around them. Whether they are interested enough to adopt it themselves, or to encourage their children to pick it up from their schoolfellows, is another question. It is hard to defend the 'Asswaree-say' into which Broad Norfolk has degenerated in industrial Norwich.

I should like true Norfolk to survive because of its expressive vocabulary and vivid turn of phrase—so much more vigorous (and honest) than the gobbledegook of the bureaucrats and sociologists, with which we are nowadays so smothered that language itself is in danger of losing its meaning. The English country dialects, if they do indeed remain alive, may well become the last repository—outside of old books—of good plain English. And yet I feel uncomfortable when people talk of 'preserving' Broad Norfolk, and organize competitions in speaking dialect. I ask myself whether, when a dialect becomes so self-conscious, it can possibly remain a genuine dialect and not an affectation.

I have never forgotten a rebuke I once received from a man who was, at the time I knew him, a journalist of some distinction both in this country and America—a friend of H. L. Mencken, the author of *The American Language*. I happened to use the word 'fulfer'.

Herbert Seaman said: 'Where did you learn that word?'

I said, 'I learnt it when I was about eight years old, from a boy who used to help in my father's garden.'

He said, 'Grr! I can speak better Norfolk than you can. You see, I *was* a gardener's boy.'

GLOSSARY

GLOSSARY

The following is a list of Norfolk words, many of which are still current today, and all of which I believe to have been in use within the past fifty years. By no means all of them are peculiar to East Anglia—some are also to be found in other English dialects, but they nevertheless form part of our Norfolk language.

Abbreviations: n. = noun; adj. = adjective; v. = verb; v.i. = intransitive verb; v.t. = transitive verb; adv. = adverb; conj. = conjunction; suff. = suffix.

A

Aberdevine (n.)	Old cage-bird-fanciers' name for siskin.
Accordin-lie (adv.)	Accordingly—with the emphasis on the last syllable. A favourite word in Norfolk. 'Accordin-*lie* to him.'
Ackulster (n.)	Axle.
Addle (v.i.)	To thrive.
Aftermath (n.)	The feed left on meadows after mowing; second crop.
A-huh (adv.)	Awry or aslant. 'All of a-huh.'
Allen/ollands (n.)	Old grassland, newly broken up.
Anend (adv.)	On end. 'Raise that ladder up anend.'
Arsle (v.)	To move or wriggle backwards.
Athwart (adv.)	Across.
Avels (n.)	Beards or awns of barley.
Ax (v.t. and i.)	Ask.

B

Bab (v.i.)	To fish for eels with a bunch of worms strung on worsted.
Backstrike (adv.)	To plough backstrike is to plough land already turned, so that it is turned back again.
Backus (n.)	Scullery or outhouse.
Badget (n.)	Badger.
Balk (n.)	A ridge of land left unploughed.
Bandy (n.)	A hare.
Bandy-wicket (n.)	Old name for cricket.
Bargood (n.)	Yeast.
Barleysel (n.)	Season of sowing barley.
Barrow-pig (n.)	The smallest pig in a litter (*See also* petman.)

Bavins (n.)	Light, loose faggots.
Bay-duck (n.)	The shelduck.
Beat (v.t.)	To mend fishing-nets. Hence 'beatster'—a net-mender.
Beaver (n.)	Farm-worker's afternoon snack.
Beck (n.)	Brook or rivulet.
Beetle (n.)	Heavy wooden hammer or mallet.
Beezlins (n.)	Cow's first milk after calving.
Begone (adj.)	Decayed, worn out.
Bents (n.)	Coarse, rushy grass.
Bestow (v.t. and i.)	(1) To lay up, put away. (2) To put a woman to bed for childbirth.
Bezzle (v.t. and i.)	(1) To drink greedily. (2) To blunt or turn the edge of a tool.
Bibble (v.i.)	To eat like a duck dabbling in mud.
Biffins (n.)	Hard, long-keeping apples, formerly reckoned a winter delicacy when baked slowly under a weight, and eaten cold with sugar and cream.
Bishy-barneybee (n.)	Ladybird.
Blar (v.i.)	Cry. Said of children—or animals. 'He blar'd like a bull.'
Blee (v.t.)	To resemble. 'How that booy du blee his father.'
Blood ulf (n.)	Bullfinch.
Boke (n.)	Bulk. 'There's more boke than corn in that crop.'
Boodle (n.)	The corn marigold.
Bop (v.t. and i.)	To duck one's head.
Bor (n.)	The universal Norfolk form of address to males. Sometimes also addressed to women, who are, however, more commonly 'maw' or 'mawther'.
Bosky (adj.)	Tipsy.
Bottle-bump (n.)	Bittern.
Bottle-nose (n.)	Porpoise.
Botty (adj.)	Fussy, self-important. 'He's a botty little man.'
Braiding (v.t.)	Net-making.
Brashy (adj.)	Land overgrown with rushes.
Brattlings (n.)	Loppings from felled trees.
Brief (n.)	Written petition handed round a village on behalf of someone in want or bereaved.
Broaches/brotches (n.)	Hazel rods sharpened at both ends and bent double—used to fasten down thatch.
Broads (n.)	The Norfolk lakes, now known to have been formed by peat-digging in the river valleys between the ninth and thirteenth centuries.
Broom-squire (n.)	Maker of birch and heather brooms.
Brumbles (n.)	Brambles.
Brush (v.t. and i.)	(1) To cut weeds with a scythe. (2) To trim a hedge. Hence 'brushings'—hedge trimmings. (3) 'Going a-brushing' means beating up game for a shoot.

Buckhead (v.t.)	To cut off the top of an overgrown hedge.
Buffle (v.i.)	To handle clumsily.
Bulk (v.i.)	To throb.
Bull's noon (n.)	Midnight.
Bumbaste (v.t.)	To beat severely.
Bumble-footed (adj.)	Clumsy.
Bunny (n.)	A bruise or swelling.
Bunt (v.t.)	To butt.
Burr (n.)	Haze round the moon.
Buskins (n.)	Leather leggings.
Butt (n.)	A flounder.

C

Caddow (n.)	Jackdaw.
Camping (n.)	Primitive game of football, now obsolete, but commemorated in the Camping Land at Swaffham.
Canker (or **redweed**) (n.)	Field poppy.
Carney (v.i.)	To wheedle, flatter, fawn upon.
Carnser (n.)	Marsh causeway.
Carr (n.)	Clump of trees by riverside or in marshland.
Cavings (n.)	Refuse from threshing.
Chaps (n.)	Cheeks—human or pigs'.
Chates (n.)	Scraps of food.
Cheat (n.)	Detachable shirt front, dicky.
Chitterlings (n.)	Pigs' entrails, cleaned and fried.
Claggy (adj.)	Moist and sticky.
Clammed (adj.)	Hungry.
Clamp (n.)	Heap of potatoes or beet, covered with straw and earth to keep out frost.
Clarty (adj.)	Daubed with syrup or juice.
Clever (adj.)	Has a special meaning in Norfolk of handsome or dexterous.
Clinkers (n.)	Small paving-bricks, set on edge.
Clout (n.)	A blow.
Clunch (n.)	Hard chalk, used in North and West Norfolk as a building material.
Clung (adj.)	Stale, limp, shrivelled.
Cob (n.)	A horse inland, but a seagull on the coast.
Cobbles (n.)	(1) Round pebbles used for building or paving. (2) Plum or cherry stones.
Colder (n.)	Refuse consisting of husks, chaff, and broken straw.
Come-back (n.)	Guinea-fowl.
Coney land (n.)	Land fit for nothing but rabbits.
Cop (v.t.)	(1) To catch anybody or anything. (2) To toss or throw.

Coquilles (n.)	Spiced buns eaten on Shrove Tuesday.
Cosh (n.)	Stick or whip.
Cosh (v.t.)	To thrash.
Couch/cag-handed (adj.)	Left-handed.
Crome (n.)	Rake with curved prongs, for drawing weeds out of ditches. Also 'muck-crome', for spreading manure; 'turnip-crome' for feeding turnips to stock.
Crook (v.t.)	To kill.
Crowd (v.t.)	To push.
Cubelow (n.)	Cupola, chimney of a malting.
Custard (n.)	A smack or blow.
Cut (n.)	A picture.
Cuter (n.)	Money.
Cyprus cat (n.)	Tabby cat. The even more curious 'calimanco cat', for tortoiseshell cat, is now obsolete.

D

Dag (n.)	Dew.
Daggly (adj.)	(1) Damp. (2) Ragged.
Dam (n.)	Stretch of marshes (e.g. Haddiscoe Dam, Gillingham Dam).
Damnified (adj.)	Indemnified. 'That ent no matters to him. He's damnified.'
Dannocks (n.)	Hedger's gloves.
Dast (v.i.)	Dare.
Dauber (n.)	Builder in wattle and daub (i.e. a mixture of clay and straw, strengthened with laths or hazel rods).
Deen (n.)	Sound. (Mother to child: 'Dornt yew dast make a deen.')
Denes (n.)	Sandy tracts on the coast.
Devilin (n.)	The swift.
Dibles (n.)	Difficulties, embarrassments.
Dick-a-dilver (n.)	Periwinkle.
Dickey (n.)	Donkey.
Didapper (n.)	Little grebe or dabchick.
Diddicoy (n.)	Gipsy. Derived from the Romany word *didecai*, which in fact means a vagrant who is no true gipsy.
Didle (n.)	Spade used for ditching.
Dindle (n.)	Sow thistle.
Ding (n.)	A blow. 'I gan him a ding o' the lug.'
Dissables (n.)	From *deshabille*. 'In his dissables' means half-dressed, or in his rough clothes.
Doddy/hoddy-doddy (adj.)	Short in stature.
Dodman (n.)	Snail.
Doke (n.)	Dent.
Dop-a-low (adj.)	Short-legged.

Doss (v.t.)	To toss.
Dow (n.)	Dove, pigeon.
Drant (v.i.)	To drawl.
Drug (n.)	Four-wheeled carriage for transporting tree-trunks.
Dudder (v.i.)	To shiver.
Duller (n.)	Noise.
Dumduckerdumer (n.)	Mixture of colours so faded as to be indescribable.
Dunnock (n.)	Hedge-sparrow. (Also known as a 'hedge accentor'.)
Dutfin (n.)	Bridle of a cart-horse.
Dwainy (adj.)	Sickly.
Dwile (n.)	Floor-cloth.

E

Ea/eau (n.)	Artificial watercourse (Fens).
Er (suff.)	When things improve in Norfolk they get 'better and betterer'—or on the contrary they may get 'worser and worserer'.
Erriwiggle (n)	Earwig.
Esh (n.)	Ash tree.

F

Fall (n.)	Veil.
Fang (v.t.)	Grab or grip. 'He fanged hold o' her arm.'
Fapes (n.)	Green gooseberries.
Fare (v.i.)	To be, feel, or seem. 'That fare as if that'll rain today.' 'I dornt fare very well.'
Farrisee (n.)	Fairy.
Fat-hen (n.)	Goose-foot weed.
Fathom (n.)	Measure of a bundle of reeds for thatching.
Fathom (v.i.)	To spread or fill out. 'The wheat fare to fathom well.'
Faut (n.)	Fault.
Ficety (adj.)	Fusty.
Fierce (adj.)	Used to describe a state of health. 'I dornt feel very fierce' means 'I don't feel well.'
Filler/thiller (n.)	The shaft horse in a team.
Fillister (n.)	Carpenter's tool used for cutting grooves or rebating.
Finnicky (adj.)	Fussy.
Firlpen (n.)	Dustpan.
Fisherate (v.i.)	To provide for. 'I can't fisherate for 'em all.'
Flag (n.)	A turf of grass.
Flag-fire (n.)	Bonfire.

Flair (v.t.)	To skin (a rabbit).
Flash (v.t.)	To trim a hedge.
Fleet (adj.)	Shallow.
Fleet (n.)	(1) A waterway (e.g. the Purfleet at Lynn). (2) Train of drift-nets paid out by a herring-boat.
Flue-boards (n.)	Barge-boards (on a house).
Fog (n.)	Long grass growing in autumn.
Foison (n.)	The juiciness of herbage. 'There's plenty of foison in this hay.'
Foreigner (n.)	Anyone not born in East Anglia.
Fosey (adj.)	Stale.
Frail (n.)	A flat rush basket.
Frame (v.i.)	To assume affected manners or speech.
Frawn (adj.)	Frozen.
Fresher (n.)	Frog.
Froise (n.)	A pancake.
Fulfer (n.)	Missel-thrush.
Fumble-fisted (adj.)	Clumsy.
Funny (adj.)	Used in the Great Yarmouth and Lowestoft districts for emphasis, as the rest of Norfolk uses 'wholly'. 'Tha's a funny big boat.' 'Tha's a funny cold day.'
Furrow-chuck (n.)	Whinchat.
Fy out (v.t.)	Short for 'bottomfy'. To fy out a ditch means to clean it out.

G

Gain (adj.)	Handy, dexterous.
Gallusdroply (adj.)	Evil-looking, foul-mouthed. 'That there diddicoy looked right gallusdroply.'
Galver (v.i.)	To throb (of a wound or abscess).
Gang (n.)	(1) A set. 'A gang of harrows.' (2) A group or team of men. 'Threshing gang.'
Gant (n.)	A village fair.
Garp (v.i.)	To gape.
Gartless (adj.)	Thoughtless.
Gast (adj.)	Barren. 'A gast mare.'
Gat (n.)	A gap or channel between the sands of the East Coast.
Gavel (n.)	(1) A sheaf of corn before it is tied up. (2) A bundle of straw for a thatcher.
Gays (n.)	Pictures in a book.
Going (n.)	Right of pasture on a common.
Golden drop (n.)	Yellow plum.
Goof/gooft (n.)	Corn-rick laid up in a barn.
Gotch (n.)	Large jug.

Go-to-bed-at-noon (n.)	Goatsbeard.
Grain (v.t.)	To strangle.
Grizzle (v.i.)	To cry querulously.
Gurn (v.i.)	To grin.

H

Ha and hacker (v.i.)	To stammer.
Hain (v.t. and i.)	To heighten; to raise wages or prices. A man who has had a rise says, 'I're been hained.'
Hakes (n.)	Hooks from which cooking-pots were hung.
Haller (v.i.)	To shout.
Hamper (v.t.)	To damage.
Hand of pork (n.)	The shoulder-joint cut without the blade-bone.
Hap (v.t.)	To wrap.
Harnser (n.)	Heron.
Harwich (n.)	'All up at Harwich' means 'in confusion'.
Hassock (n.)	Tussock of coarse grass.
Hayjack (n.)	Whitethroat. (Signifying that it makes its nest of hay or straw.)
Haysel (n.)	Haymaking-time.
Haze (v.t.)	To dry linen by hanging it in the open.
Hedgeman (n.)	Hedge-sparrow.
Hen's noseful (n.)	A very small quantity.
Herne (n.)	Part of one parish projecting into another.
Higgle (v.i.)	To bargain or haggle.
Highlows (n.)	Ankle boots.
High sprites (n.)	Ghosts.
Himp (v.i.)	To limp.
Hinder (adv.)	Hither. 'Cop it inter holl, bor. Hinder come a dow.'
Hinder (adj.)	(1) Rear. 'The hinder legs' of a horse. (2) Near. 'The hinder side' of the barn, as distinct from the 'yon' (far) side.
Hips (n.)	The corners of a stack.
Hitch (v.i.)	Shift. 'Hitch up a bit', on a crowded bench.
Hobby (n.)	A horse or pony.
Hock (v.t.)	To trip.
Hogget (n.)	A sheep after the first shearing.
Hold (v.i.)	To have money. 'Do you hold today?' means 'Have you any money today?'
Holl (n.)	Ditch—usually a dry ditch.
Hollow meat (n.)	Rabbit or poultry, as distinct from butcher's meat.
Horfling (v.i.)	Moving awkwardly.

Horn-pie (n.)	Lapwing.
Hostrees (n.)	Fastenings to which the whippletrees (draw-bars) are fastened on ploughs or harrows.
Hot pot (n.)	Warmed ale and spirits—usually old ale and gin.
Howsomever (conj.)	However.
Huckabuck (n.)	Leapfrog.
Hulk (v.t.)	To gut (a rabbit or hare).
Hull (v.t.)	To hurl, throw.
Hulver (n.)	Holly.
Hummer (n.)	A lie.
Hunch (n.)	A push or shove.
Hutch (n.)	A chest or cupboard.
Hutkin (n.)	Finger-stall.
Huxterer (n.)	Dealer.

I

Imitate (v.t. and i.)	In Norfolk, means to attempt. 'I shoun't imitate to do that if I was you.'

K

Kail (v.t.)	To throw.
Kelter (n.)	Condition. 'That farm look in good kelter.'
Kewter (n.)	Money.
Killer/keeler (n.)	A shallow tub, cooler.
King Harry (n.)	Goldfinch.
Kiss-me-at-the-garden-gate (n.)	Pansy.
Kit (n.)	Fish-basket. A boat is said to have landed so many kit of soles, plaice, etc.
Kitty witch (n.)	Seagull, kittiwake.
Knap (v.t.)	To knock or tap. Flint-knapping (splitting flints to give them a smooth surface) is an ancient and peculiarly East Anglian craft.
Knap-kneed (adj.)	Knock-kneed.
Know (n.)	Knowledge. 'He told me all his know.'

L

Lad's love (n.)	The herb southernwood.
Lady's smock (n.)	Cuckoo flower, Canterbury bell.
Laid (v.t.)	Corn is 'laid' (flattened) by heavy rain or gales.

Lam (v.t.)	To beat.
Lambs' tails (n.)	Willow catkins.
Lanner (n.)	Whiplash.
Largees (n.)	Bounty or tip to harvesters.
Lashy (adj.)	Soft, watery.
Last (n.)	Ten long hundreds (132) of herrings.
Latch (v.i.)	To catch. 'His coat got latched in the barb-wire.'
Ligger (n.)	(1) Plank bridge over a ditch. (2) Float, made of a bunch of reeds, for pike-fishing.
'Lijahs (n.)	Straps round the trousers, just below the knee.
Lints (n.)	Fishing nets.
Lode (n.)	Artificial watercourse (Fens).
Loke (n.)	A blind alley or lane.
Lucom (n.)	(1) Dormer-window. (2) Roof of a hoist outside a warehouse or mill.
Lug (n.)	Ear.
Lummox (n.)	A heavy, clumsy person. 'Git yew out o' the way, yer great lummox!'

M

Malted (adj.)	Hot and sweating.
Mardle (n. and v.i.)	(1) Pond. (2) To gossip.
Marl (n.)	Chalk or chalky clay, formerly dug out of pits and spread on the land as a fertilizer—hence, 'marl-pit'.
Marram (n.)	Coarse, reedy grass growing on sand-dunes. Hence the term 'marrams' for the dunes themselves.
Mash/mesh (n.)	Marsh.
Master (adj.)	Expresses admiration. 'Tha's a master great house, that is.'
Masterpiece (n.)	Anything astonishing. 'Well, I shoun't never ha' believed it. Tha's a masterpiece!'
Matchly (adj.)	Exactly alike, fitting well.
Mavis/mavish (n.)	Song-thrush.
Mawkin (n.)	Scarecrow.
Mawther (n.)	Woman or girl—feminine equivalent of 'bor'.
Mazy (adj.)	(1) Sickly or unwholesome. (2) Description of shotten or inferior herrings.
Meals (n.)	Sand-dunes.
Mellow (adj.)	Ripe.
Midnight woman (n.)	Midwife.
Million (n.)	Melon or pumpkin.
Minify (v.t.)	To make little of—opposite of magnify.
Misery (n.)	Pain. 'She suffer with a misery in har stommick.'
Mislen-bush (n.)	Mistletoe.

71

Mite (n.)	A little bit. 'I dorn't fare a mite hungry.'
Mock (v.t.)	To place irregularly.
Moise (v.i.)	To thrive, get better. 'Them bullocks dorn't fare to moise.'
Monge (v.t.)	To eat greedily.
Morfrey (n.)	Tumbril convertible into a wagon (=hermaphrodite).
Mouse-hunt (n.)	Stoat.
Mow in (v.i.)	Join in.
Muckwash (n.)	Sweat. 'All of a muckwash' means sweating profusely.
Mud scuppit (n.)	Scoop for cleaning out ditches.
Mure-hearted (adj.)	'Demure-', tender-hearted.

N

Nasty-particular (adj.)	Fussy.
Neatus/nettus (n.)	Cattle-shed.
Nice (adj.)	Too particular, finicky.
Nijjerting (v.i.)	Assisting in childbirth.
Nogging (n.)	Brickwork between timbers.
No matters (adj.)	'I dorn't fare no matters' means 'I don't feel very well.'
Nonicking (n.)	Horseplay.
Numbchance (adj.)	Inattentive, stupid.

O

Oat-flights (n.)	Oat chaff, formerly used by the poor to stuff pillows and mattresses.
Ollands (n.)	Old grassland, newly tilled.
Overwart (adv.)	To 'plough overwart' means to plough at right angles to the original furrows.

P

Padduck (n.)	Toad.
Page (n.)	Shepherd's boy.
Pagle (n.)	Cowslip.
Pamment (n.)	Pavement.
Pample (v.i.)	To tread lightly.
Passe (n.)	Passion. To 'get into a passe' is to fly into a temper.
Pawker (n.)	Beachcomber.
Paxwax (n.)	Sinew in a joint of meat.
Pearks (n.)	Gadgets.
Ped (n.)	(1) Pannier in which countrywomen carried their produce to market. (2) Fish-basket.

Pensy (adj.)	Fretful.
Petman (n.)	The smallest pig in a litter. (*See also* barrow-pig.)
Pick-cheese (n.)	Blue tit.
Piewipe (n.)	Peewit, lapwing.
Pightle (n.)	Paddock.
Pinpanches (n.)	Winkles.
Pishamare-barneybee (n.)	Earwig.
Pishmire/pishamare (n.)	Ant.
Plain (n.)	A town square or open space.
Plancher (n.)	Wooden floor.
Plawks (n.)	Hands.
Poddle-ladle/pollywiggle (n.)	Tadpole.
Pods (n.)	Eel-nets.
Poke (n.)	Bag or sack.
Popple (n.)	(1) Nonsense, fuss. (2) Choppy water.
Potchet (n.)	Fragment of pottery.
Pricker-bag (n.)	Dinner-bag.
Primmicky (adj.)	Affected, hard to please.
Pritch (n.)	Pointed tool (eel-pritch, fold-pritch).
Puckaterry (n.)	'In a puckaterry' means in a muddle or a temper.
Pudding poke (n.)	Long-tailed tit—so called from the shape of its nest.
Pulk (n.)	Small pond or pool.
Pummace (n.)	The pulp left after apples have been crushed for cider.
Push (n.)	A boil or carbuncle.

Q

Quackle (v.t.)	To choke or strangle.
Quant (n. and v.t.)	(1) The Norfolk Broads version of a punt pole. (2) To push a wherry, yacht, or gun punt with a quant.
Queer (adj.)	'Feeling queer' means feeling ill.

R

Rabbit (v.i.)	In carpentry—to rebate or cut grooves.
Rafty (adj.)	Of weather—damp, raw, and misty.
Rally (n.)	A shelf built into a wall.
Ranny (n.)	Shrew-mouse.
Rare (adj.)	Used for emphasis—'Tha's rarely hot today', 'He's a rare tall man.'
Raw (adj.)	Angry. 'He was wholly raw.'
Reasty (adj.)	Rancid.
Reel-a-bobbin (n.)	Cotton-reel.

73

Rent (n. and v.t.)	Tear. 'He're got a rent in his breeches', or 'She're rent her skirt on a brumble.'
Ringes (n.)	Rows of plants.
Roarers/roaring boys (n.)	Men who shovelled herrings and salt together.
Roger (n.)	A whirlwind.
Roke (n.)	Fog.
Roment (v.)	To invent or exaggerate a story.
Rond (n.)	Reed-bed or bog between the river-bank and the water.
Room of (adv.)	Instead of.
Rorping (v.i.)	Kicking up a noise. Often said of a noisy bull: 'Hark at tha old bull a-rorpin'.'
Rows (n.)	The narrow streets or alleys (some only about four feet wide) of old Yarmouth.
Ruck (n. and v.t.)	Crease.
Run (v.i.)	To leak (said of a bucket, saucepan, or kettle). 'Dornt use that there saucepan. That run.'
Runnel (n.)	A wheel.

S

Sadly (adj.)	Unwell. 'The missus, she're been very sadly, ter year.'
Scalder (n.)	Crowd. 'There's a scalder o' rooks on the five-acre.'
Score (n.)	Steep path or lane down cliffs. (A word found chiefly in Lowestoft and Beccles.)
Scrab (v.t.)	To scratch.
Scud (v.)	To shake herrings out of the nets.
Scuppit (n.)	Scoop.
Scute (n.)	A triangular or otherwise awkward shaped part of a field.
Seal/sele (n.)	(1) Time, season. (2) Greeting. 'I gan him the seal o' the day.'
Sea-pie (n.)	Oyster-catcher.
Segs (n.)	Rushes, sedges. As in a 'seg-bottomed' (rush-bottomed) chair.
Sension (n.)	Groundsel.
Shack (n.)	Grain shaken out of the ear at harvest.
Shannock (n.)	A native of Sheringham.
Shanny (adj.)	Scatter-brained, excited. 'What ha' yew gone shanny?'
Sharm (v.i.)	To yell, scream, cry.
Shell (adj.)	Skewbald, brown and white. (Used chiefly of horses.)
Shepherd's sundial (n.)	Scarlet pimpernel.
Shim (n.)	White stripe or blaze on a horse's face.
Sheers (n.)	'The Sheers' are anywhere in England outside East Anglia' and anyone who comes from the Shires or 'from away; is a 'foreigner'.
Shiver (n.)	A splinter. 'I're got a shiver in my finger.'

Shoof (n.)	Sheaf.
Shrike (n.)	Butcher bird.
Shruck (v.i.)	Past tense of 'shriek'. 'She shruck out.'
Shruff (n.)	Bits of stick and twigs, used for firing.
Shywanicking (n.)	Boisterous frolic.
Sibrits (n.)	Banns.
Sight (n.)	A great number. 'There was a sight of folk there.'
Silly-bold (adj.)	Impudent.
Sisserara (n.)	A hard blow, or a scolding.
Skep (n.)	Big wicker basket used on farm or in garden.
Skrowge (v.i.)	Crowd together, squeeze, push.
Slad (n.)	(1) Hollow between two hills. (2) Flooded marsh where wild duck feed.
Slarver (v.i. and n.)	(1) To dribble (saliva), drool. (2) To talk inconsequentially.
Slop (n.)	Smock or apron.
Slug-horn (n.)	Stunted, down-turned horn in cattle.
Slummocking (adj.)	Gawky, untidy. 'A slummockin' great mawther.'
Sluss (n.)	Slush.
Smeath (n.)	Large, open level of land (*e.g.* Markham Smeath—scene of famous Swaffham coursing meeting).
Smee (n.)	Young wild duck.
Smittick (n.)	Tiny piece.
Smur (n.)	Drizzle.
Snack (n.)	Latch.
Snarl (n. and v.t.)	Tangle.
Sneerfroys (adj.)	Supercilious.
Snob (n.)	Shoemaker.
Sole (v.t.)	To beat.
Soler (n.)	A big one. 'Tha's a soler, that is.'
Soller (n.)	Loft.
Sosh/soshens (adj.)	'On the sosh', or 'soshens', means slanting, sideways, or out of line.
Sow (n.)	Wood-louse, millipede.
Spantry (n.)	Threshold—also, 'troshel'.
Spars (n.)	Rafters.
Spink (n.)	Chaffinch.
Splaar (v.t.)	To spread.
Spolt (adj.)	Crisp, brittle.
Sprung (adj.)	Split.
Spud (n.)	Weeding tool on the end of a stick.
Spuffle (v.i.)	To fuss, speak pompously.
Squinny (adj.)	Lank, thin.
Squit (n.)	Nonsense. 'Dorn't talk squit.'
Stag (n.)	Cock turkey.
Staithe (n.)	Quay, landing-place.
Stam (v.t.)	To astonish.

Stank/stanch (n.)	Dam.
Stannicle (n.)	Stickleback.
Stewkey blues (n.)	Cockles fished off Stiffkey.
Stewping (v.i.)	Drinking noisily.
Stingy (adj.)	(1) Mean, cruel. (2) Very cold. 'Stingy old weather.'
Stive (n.)	Dust. 'Dorn't kick up a stive.'
Stover (n.)	Winter food for cattle.
Strammacking (n.)	Gadding about.
Strong-docked (adj.)	Thickset about the loins and rump.
Stroop (n.)	Windpipe, gullet.
Sue (v.i.)	To issue, discharge (of a wound or abscess).
Sukey (n.)	A hare.
Sunket (n.)	A little (of food).
Swalacking (v.i.)	Sweltering.
Swale (n.)	Shade.
Swidge (n.)	Puddle.
Swill (n.)	Basket containing 500 herrings.
Swoddy (n.)	Soldier.

T

Ta/ter (article or pronoun)	The, this, that, or it. 'Ta fare to rain pourin'.' 'Ter year'—this year.
Tempest (n.)	Thunderstorm.
Tetter (n.)	Pimple.
Thack (v.t.)	(1) To thatch. (2) To thrash.
Tidy (adj.)	Good, fair. 'Tha's a tidy long way to Norwich.'
Tiller (v.i.)	To throw out many stems from a root. 'The barley fare to tiller well.'
Time (adv.)	While. 'I watched him time he was a-duin' on it.'
Tit-lark (n.)	Meadow pipit.
Tittermatorter (n.)	See-saw.
Titty-totty (adj.)	Very small.
Tizzick (n.)	Cough.
Tricolate (v.t.)	To adorn or repair. 'He're tricolated that house up a treat.'
Trosh (v.t.)	To thresh.
Troshel (n.)	Threshold.
Twizzle (v.t. and i.)	To twist or spin quickly.

U

Unean (adv.)	Underneath.
Ungain (adj.)	Clumsy.

V

Vacagees (n.) Wartime evacuees.

W

Warmin (n.) Vermin. Ill-behaved person or animal.
Wetshed (adj.) To be wetshed means to get your feet wet.
Whelm (v.t.) (1) To turn a bucket or other utensil upside down. (2) To throw out the contents.
Wherry (n.) The distinctive Norfolk Broads sailing-barge, with a single huge black sail.
Whifflers (n.) Attendants who cleared the way for Norwich Corporation processions on Guild Days.
Whippletree (n.) The draw-bar to which the horses' traces were attached on a plough or harrow.
Wholly (adv.) Used for emphasis. 'She was wholly scared' means she was very frightened.
Widdles (n.) Pimples.
Winnicking (v.i.) Whimpering.
Winnol weather (n.) Stormy weather around 3 March, which is the Festival of St Winwaloe, a British saint.
First come David, then come Chad;
Then come Winnol, blowing like mad.
Wittery (adj.) Weak.
Wittles (n.) Food (victuals).
Wry (n.) Mistake (*e.g.* praise of a newly knitted pair of socks: 'There ain't a wry in 'em, not nowhere').

Y

Yalm (v.t.) To eat. 'He yalmed that into him.'
Yard (n.) Cottage garden.
Yarwhelp (n.) Black-tailed godwit.
Yelk (n.) Yolk of an egg.
Yoke (v.t.) To harness (farm-horses).
Yow (v.i.) To howl (e.g. to a fretful child during a meal: 'Ivery time yew yow yew lose a chow').

More books of Local Interest

A Prospect of Norwich

A picture of Norwich from the late 17th to mid-19th centuries through the eyes of
some of the leading figures of the Norwich School of Artists. The Castle, Cathedral,
River, Churches and Chapels, City Walls and Gates, and Public Buildings are
depicted in a series of delightful prints and engravings accompanied by a lively and
informative text by Norwich writer George Nobbs.

A welcome and unusual book for all those who love Norwich.
Available in hardback at £9.95, paperback at £7.95

The Best of Jonathan Mardle

A collection of essays about Norfolk by Eric Fowler, writing as Jonathan Mardle.
Peter Roberts, former editor of the *Eastern Daily Press* said of him 'he achieved the
distinction of having thousands and thousands of friends right through the region,
who never met him but gathered comfort, stimulation and provocation from all the
articles that appeared from his pen. In fact he told people what he believed to be
right and did it in prose of compelling clarity and sincerity'.
This superb collection also contains delightful illustrations by Irene Ogden.

Available in hardback £9.95

The Boy John Letters

The complete series of Sidney Grapes' famous 'Boy John Letters',
re-published by the Mousehold Press, in association with Prospect Press,
with an appreciation by Keith Skipper.

ISBN 1 874739 29 3   £9.95

Also available on C.D., Keith Skipper reads a selection of the Boy John Letters,
with Sheilah Olley as Aunt Agatha

ISBN 1 874739 30 7   £9.95

Printed in Great Britain by
St Edmundsbury Press Ltd, Bury St Edmunds, Suffolk